Real Time English

Student Book

Contents

Overview of the course

Real Time English is a language course intended for beginning level students who wish to use English as a language for communication. The goal of *Real Time English* is to teach students basic communicative language skills, through careful presentation of grammar and vocabulary and through a gradual progression of speaking and listening exercises.

Real Time English consists of this Student Book, classroom audio cassettes, and a Teacher's Manual. The Student Book contains an Introduction Unit, 12 main units, and Classroom Notes for the teacher. Each of the nine *Presentation Units* (1, 2, 3, 5, 6, 7, 9, 10, 11) presents new grammar points, vocabulary items, listening and speaking exercises, and social exchange formulas. Each of the three *Challenge Units* (4, 8, 12) presents grammar revision exercises and interaction activities.

Organization of the course

The course consists of 12 main units, plus an Introduction Unit. The Classroom Notes, in the back of the textbook for teacher reference, provide additional Warm Up and Follow Up activities. Each of the five sections of a unit requires 30-45 minutes of class time. As such, *Real Time English* provides approximately 36 hours of work. When expansion, review, and self-study activities are utilized, *Real Time English* provides a minimum of 48 hours of work.

Introduction Unit

The Introduction Unit provides basic language needed to begin the course. The Introduction Unit gives listening and speaking practice with letters, numbers, colors, clock times, days, months, years, and some helpful classroom expressions.

Presentation Units (1, 2, 3, 5, 6, 7, 9, 10, 11)

Each presentation unit contains these sections:

First Try—a presentation of grammar points in short, model conversations and two open-ended exchanges for practice

Word Bank—a presentation of vocabulary items in a visual context, with a series of exercises to help learn new words

Listening—a set of three types of listening exercises:

> *Easy Listening*—a series of items to check aural comprehension of new grammar and vocabulary

> *Listening Dictation*—a set of fill-in items to check aural perception of new grammar

> *Listening Task*—a selective listening exercise to develop comprehension of functional language

Pair Practice—an interactive exercise to develop both grammatical accuracy and speaking fluency

Social Talk—a presentation and practice of formulaic language commonly used in social settings

Challenge Units (4, 8, 12)

After every three presentation units, there is a Challenge Unit. Each of these units contains exercises for reviewing, consolidating, and expanding the material of the previous lessons. The Challenge Units are intended to be more open than the presentation units in order to allow the students to integrate and apply what they have been studying.

Each Challenge Unit contains a combination of these sections:

Conversation Review: These tables help students to review the structure of the conversations they have practiced.

Grammar Review: These exercises help students review question forms, sentence formation, and word order.

Vocabulary Activities: These exercises help students activate the words and expressions they have been learning.

Interaction Games: These games allow the students to use the language they have studied and also to enjoy interaction in English.

Classroom Notes

At the back of the book are Classroom Notes for the teacher. These notes give basic classroom procedures for each section of *Real Time English*. The notes also offer extra warm up and follow up exercises for each section of every unit so that teachers may challenge their students by expanding the activities of the book. The Classroom Notes are divided into two sections: Teaching Procedures and Unit Notes.

Audio Cassettes

All of the material for the First Try conversation models, Word Bank presentations, Listening exercises, and Social Talk sections are recorded on audio tape. These audio tapes are available separately.

Teacher's Manual

A separate Teacher's Manual contains detailed teaching notes, as well as answer keys for the Student Book exercises, and the Tapescript for the Word Bank and Listening sections.

Basic Tools

1. Letters of the alphabet

Listen and repeat.

A a	B b	C c	D d	E e	F f
G g	H h	I i	J j	K k	L l
M m	N n	O o	P p	Q q	R r
S s	T t	U u	V v	W w	X x
Y y	Z z				

Say your name. Then spell your name.

2. Numbers

Listen and repeat.

1	2	3	4	5	6	7	8	9	10
11	12	13	14	15	16	17	18	19	20
25	30	35	40	45	50	55	60	65	70
75	80	85	90	95	100	150	155	199	200
1000									

Look at these numbers. Say them.

2   7   11   14   21   39   44   59   66

72   83   99   101   234   529   667   925

3. Colors

Listen and repeat.

Basic colors:

white   black   gray   brown   red   orange   yellow   green   blue   pink

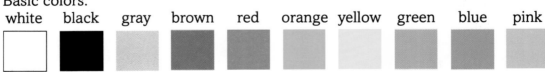

What color is it? Say the color.

4. Time

Listen and repeat.

7:00   7:15   7:30   7:45 a.m.   7:50 p.m.   12:00 noon   12:00 midnight

What time is it? Say the time.

5. Days

Listen and repeat.

Sunday   Monday   Tuesday   Wednesday   Thursday   Friday   Saturday

What day is the 2nd (second)?
It's a Tuesday.
Say these days:

1st (first)   3rd (third)   6th (sixth)

11th (eleventh)   20th (twentieth)

25th (twenty-fifth)

S	M	T	W	Th	F	S
	1	2	3	4	5	6
7	8	9	10	11	12	13
14	15	16	17	18	19	20
20	21	22	23	24	25	26
27	28	29	30			

6. Months

Listen and repeat.

January   February   March   April   May   June

July   August   September   October   November   December

What month is it? Say the month.

7. Years

Listen and repeat.

1970 Nineteen seventy
1979 Nineteen seventy-nine
1990 Nineteen ninety
1993 Nineteen ninety-three
2000 Two thousand
2010 Twenty ten

Say the year.

1925	1941	1952	1963
1977	1980	1992	1999

8. Dates

Listen and repeat.

Monday, January 15th, 1992   Wednesday, August 1st, 1975
Friday, December 3rd, 1982   Sunday, December 31st, 1999

Say these dates.

Mon – 1/25/92   Wed – 3/19/95   Fri – 12/21/96   Sun – 6/15/97

9. Classroom expressions

Listen and repeat.

Please repeat that.

I'm sorry. I don't understand.

Excuse me. I have a question.

What does __ mean?

How do you say __ in English?

What's this?

Sorry, I don't know.

What's this in English?

How do you spell that?

How do you pronounce that?

Could you say that again, please?

First Try

1. Pronunciation

Listen and repeat.

> Hello.   Hi.   Good morning.   How are you?
>
> My name's Mark Smith.   Nice to meet you.

2. Work in pairs

First listen to the conversations. Then practice in pairs.

1.

Hello, Beth.
Hello, Alex.

2.

Good morning, Ms. Jackson.
Hi, Beth. How are you?

3.

Hello. My name's Mark Adams.
Hi, I'm Sarah Parker.

4.

Hello. I'm Karen.
Hi, I'm Andy.
Nice to meet you.
Nice to meet you, too.

3. Let's try it

Complete these conversations.

1.

Hello, _____.
Hi, _____.

2.

Hello, I'm _____.
Hi, I'm _____.
_____ to meet _____.
_____ to meet _____, too.

Word Bank 📼

Listen and look at the pictures. Then repeat the words.

Nationality

American	British	Australian	Mexican	Brazilian
French	German	Japanese	Chinese	Korean

Family

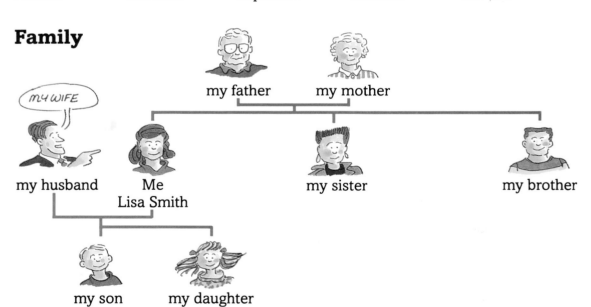

MY WIFE

my father   my mother

my husband   Me
Lisa Smith   my sister   my brother

my son   my daughter

Address

Ken Kimura
240 South Main Street
Los Angeles California 90011
USA

Phone number

G Maria Gomez
(213) 975-6843

1. Nationality

Complete the words.

1.

Steffi Graf
She's G_____

2.

Madonna
She's A_____

3.

Crown Prince Naruhito
and Princess Masako
They're J_____

4.

Jacques Cousteau
He's F_____

5.

Prince Charles and
Princess Diana
They're B_____

6.

Mel Gibson
He's A_____

2. Family

Look at the Hill family tree. Say how the people are related.

Tom — Sue
Mary — Jack
Willie — Sally

1. Tom – Sue   Tom is Sue's _____.
2. Tom – Mary   Tom is Mary's _____.
3. Mary – Jack   Mary is Jack's _____.
4. Sally – Willie   Sally is Willie's _____.

3. How about you?

Ask your partner.

What's your name?
What's your nationality? (Where are you from?)
What's your address? (Where do you live?)
What's your phone number?

Name _____
Address _____
_____
_____
Nationality _____
Phone number _____

New Words

Do you know more words?

Nationality

_____

Family

_____

UNIT ONE

Listening

1. Easy listening

Check (✓) the correct picture.

1.

   ☑ Mark   ❑ Mary

2.

   ❑ Wife   ❑ Sister

3.

   ❑   ❑

4.

   ❑   ❑

5.

   ❑   ❑

6.

   ❑   ❑

2. Listening dictation

Listen. Write the words.

Is she   Are you   I'm   She's   They're   she isn't
they aren't   Are   is Chinese   my brother   No

1. This is Rumi Sato. ___She's___ Japanese.

2. This is Peter. He's _____ _____.

3. _____ _____ Korean?

   No, _____ _____. *She*_____ _____.

4. _____ Peter and Anna American?

   No, _____ _____. _____ *German.*

5. _____ _____ American?

   _____, *I'm not.* _____ *Mexican.*

3. Listening task

Listen. Which picture? Write the numbers on the pictures.

Pair Practice A

Student A look at this page. Student B look at page 8.

Language Key	
Ask	**Answer**
Is Lucy Spanish?	Yes, she is. *or* No, she isn't. She's Italian.
How old is Lucy?	She's 19 years old.

Ask your partner. Write the information.

1. Mario Conti

   He is _____.
   Italian or Spanish
   He is _____ years old.
   24 or 27

2. Jung-Ja Kim

   She is _____.
   Korean or Chinese
   She is 26 years old.

3. Anna Hong

   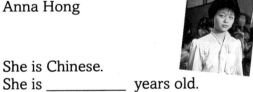

   She is Chinese.
   She is _____ years old.
   26 or 28

4. David Perez

   He is Mexican.
   He is 35 years old.

5. Peter Brand

   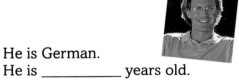

   He is German.
   He is _____ years old.
   32 or 42

6. Mari Asaka

   She is Japanese.
   She is _____ years old.
   31 or 33

- -

EXTRA! EXTRA!

Talk to your partner. Ask five questions:

- What's your name?
- How many people are in your family?
- How old are you?
- What's your nationality?
- What's your favorite movie?
- How old are you?
- What's your address?
- What's your phone number?
- *Your own question*

Social Talk—Greetings

1. Listen in

Listen to the conversations.

1.

Hi, Maria.

Hi, Anna. How are you?

Fine.

2.

Good morning, class.

Good morning, Mr. Park.

3.

Good morning. How are you?

Fine. How are you?

Great.

4.

Hello.

Hi. How are you today?

Fine, thanks. And you?

OK.

2. Act it out

Work in pairs. Practice the conversations.

Pair Practice B

Student B look at this page. Student A look at page 6.

Language Key	
Ask	**Answer**
Is Lucy Spanish?	Yes, she is. *or* No, she isn't. She's Italian.
How old is Lucy?	She's 19 years old.

Ask your partner. Write the information.

1. Mario Conti

   He is Italian.
   He is 24 years old.

2. Jung-Ja Kim

   She is Korean.
   She is _____ years old.
   26 or 36

3. Anna Hong

   She is _____.
   Chinese or Korean
   She is 28 years old.

4. David Perez

   He is _____.
   Mexican or Spanish
   He is _____ years old.
   25 or 35

5. Peter Brand

   He is _____.
   American or German
   He is 32 years old.

6. Mari Asaka

   She is _____.
   American or Japanese
   She is 31 years old.

EXTRA! EXTRA!

Talk to your partner. Ask five questions:

- What's your name?
- How many people are in your family?
- How old are you?
- What's your nationality?
- What's your favorite movie?
- How old are you?
- What's your address?
- What's your phone number?
- *Your own question*

First Try

1. Pronunciation

Listen and repeat.

> Is this...?   Is this your coat?   Yes, it is.   No, it isn't.
>
> Is this your bag?   No, it isn't.   My bag is brown.

2. Work in pairs

First listen to the conversations. Then practice in pairs.

1.

Is this your coat?
Yes, it is. Thank you.

2.

Is this your book?
No, it isn't.

3.

Is this your desk?   Is this your desk?
No, it isn't.   *Yes, it is.*

4.

Is this your bag?   Is this your bag?
No, it isn't. My   *Yes, it is. Thank*
bag is brown.   *you.*

3. Let's try it

Complete these conversations.

1.

Is this your _____?
No, _____ _____.
Is this _____ _____?
Yes, _____ _____.

2.

Is this your _____?
No, _____ _____.
My _____ is _____.
Is this _____ _____?
Yes, _____ _____. Thank you.

Word Bank 📼

Listen and look at the pictures. Then repeat the words.

Classroom

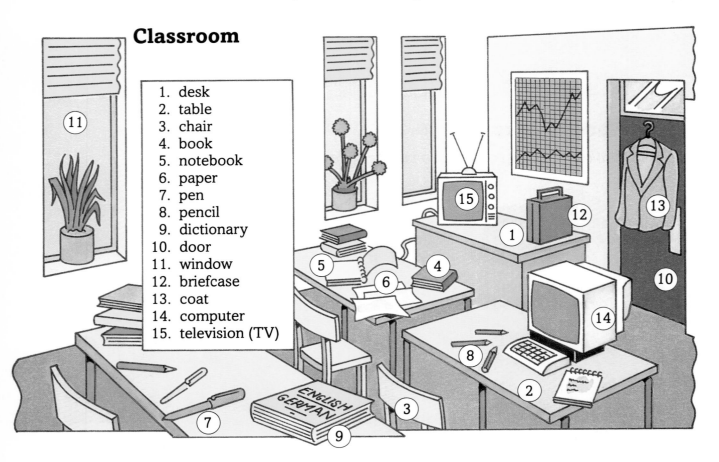

1. desk
2. table
3. chair
4. book
5. notebook
6. paper
7. pen
8. pencil
9. dictionary
10. door
11. window
12. briefcase
13. coat
14. computer
15. television (TV)

Adjectives

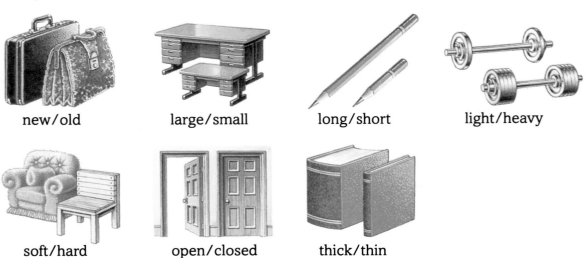

new/old   large/small   long/short   light/heavy

soft/hard   open/closed   thick/thin

1. What is it?

Ask and answer.

What is Number (1)?   *It's a chair.* or *Sorry, I don't know.*

1. a _____

2. a _____

3. a _____

4. a _____

2. How many are there?

Look at your classroom. Ask and answer.

How many students are there?   *There are 25.*

none (0)? 1?   2?   3?

1.

Students?   How many? _____

2.

Chairs?   How many? _____

3.

Desks?   How many? _____

4.

Doors?   How many? _____

5.

Windows?   How many? _____

6.

Tables?   How many? _____

3. Is this your ... ?

Each person puts three things on a table.
Then go to the table. Pick up one thing. Ask someone:

_____, is this your (book)?   *Yes, it is.*
   No, it isn't.   (It isn't my (book).)

New Words

Do you know more words?

Things in your classroom   _____

2

Listening

1. Easy listening

Listen. Check (✓) the correct picture.

1.
☐ ☐ ☐ ☐

3.
☐ ☐

4.
☐ ☐

5.
☐ ☐

6.
☐ ☐

2. Listening dictation

Listen. Write the words.

a	some	and	one	two	three	new	Tom's
His	Mary's	Her	Their	Our	room	American	

1. There are _____ books and _____ notebooks.

2. I have _____ computers and _____ tape player.

3. We have _____ desks _____ _____ table.

4. There is _____ small _____ and _____ large _____.

5. Mary has _____ blue notebook. _____ notebook is blue.

6. Tom has a new computer. _____ computer is new.

7. Ted and Marla have a new teacher. _____ teacher is _____.

8. Maria and I have a new computer. _____ computer is _____.

3. Listening task

Listen. Draw lines (——) to the correct office.

Pair Practice A

Student A look at this page. Student B look at page 16.

Language Key	
Ask	**Answer**
Is John's house large?	Yes, it is. *or* No, it isn't.

Look at the pictures numbers 1,3,5. Ask B questions. Circle the correct picture. Look at the pictures numbers 2,4,6. Answer B's questions.

1. John

large   small

2. Mary

large

3. John

old   new

4. Mary

old

5. John

big   small

6. Mary

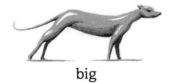

big

• •

EXTRA! EXTRA!

Who is it?

Think of a person in your class. Say:

His (coat) is (blue). *or* Her (bag) is (red).

Your partner will guess.

Is it Tom?   *No.*   Is it Yuji?   *Yes.*

Try five times.

Social Talk—Bye!

2

1. Listen in

Listen to the conversations.

1.

Bye!

Bye! Have a good day!

2.

Bye, Mark.

See you later.

3.

Goodbye, Mary. See you Monday.

Have a nice weekend.

Thanks. You too.

4.

Take care. Have a nice trip.

Thanks. Bye!

2. Act it out

Work in pairs. Practice the conversations.

UNIT TWO

Pair Practice B 👥

Student B look at this page. Student A look at page 14.

Language Key	
Ask	**Answer**
Is John's house large?	Yes, it is. *or* No, it isn't.

Look at the pictures numbers 2, 4, 6. Ask A questions. Circle the correct picture. Look at the pictures numbers 1, 3, 5. Answer A's questions.

1. John

large

2. Mary

large

small

3. John

new

4. Mary

old

new

5. John

big

6. Mary

small

big

∙∙

EXTRA! EXTRA! 👥

Who is it?

Think of a person in your class. Say:

His (coat) is (blue). *or* Her (bag) is (red).

Your partner will guess.

Is it Tom?   *No.*   Is it Yuji?   *Yes.*

Try five times.

First Try

1

2

3

4

1. Pronunciation

Listen and repeat.

> Is this...?   Are these...?   Is this your car?   Yes, it is.   No, it isn't.
>
> Are these your bags?   Yes, they are.   No, they aren't.
>
> It's a nice car.   Yes, I know. Thank you.

2. Work in pairs

First listen to the conversations. Then practice in pairs.

1.

Is this your car?
Yes, it is.
It's a nice car.
Yes, I know. Thank you.

2.

Is this your apartment?
Yes, it is.
It's a very small apartment.
Yes, I know. Sorry.

3.

Are these your bags?
Yes, they are.
They're heavy!
Yes, I know. Sorry.

4.

Are these your children?
Yes, they are.
They're very cute.
Do you think so? Thank you.

3. Let's try it

Complete these conversations.

1.

Is this your _____?
Yes, it is.
It's a _____ _____.
_____.

2.

Are these your _____?
Yes, they are.
They're very _____.
_____.

Word Bank 📼

Listen and look at the pictures. Then repeat the words.

Things at home

1. backpack
2. suitcase
3. bag
4. wallet
5. keys
6. watch

7. shirt
8. pants
9. skirt
10. sweater
11. shoes

12. car
13. bicycle

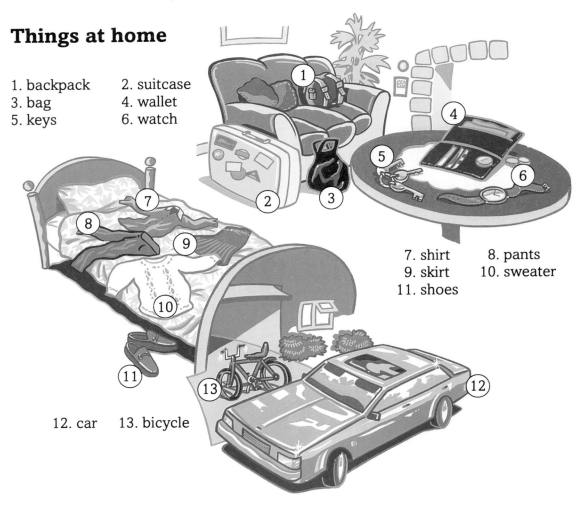

Adjectives

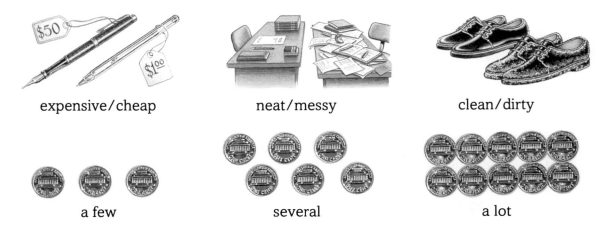

expensive/cheap   neat/messy   clean/dirty

a few   several   a lot

1. What's this?

Ask and answer.

| What's this? | It's a (coat). |
| What are these? | They're (coats). |

1.

2.

3.

4.

5.

6.

2. This—these

Ask and answer.

| Is this your (book)? | Yes, it is. |
| Are these your (books)? | Yes, they are. |

1. book?

2. books?

3. shoes?

4. bicycle?

5. suitcases?

6. keys?

3. That's a nice...

Say and answer.

| That's a nice... | Thank you. |
| Those are nice... | Thanks. |

| That's a beautiful... | Thanks. |
| Those are beautiful... | Thank you. |

New Words

Do you know more words?

Things in your home _____

UNIT THREE

Listening

1. Easy listening

Listen. Check (✓) the correct picture.

1. ❑   ❑   2. ❑   ❑

3. ❑   ❑   4. ❑   ❑

5. ❑   ❑   6. ❑   ❑

2. Listening dictation

Listen. Choose the words. Write them.

Is this	Are these	It is	They are	This is
These are	it isn't	They aren't	I have	He has
She has	You have	They have	His	Her Their

1. _____ _____ your books? *Yes, they are.*

2. _____ _____ your car? *No,* _____ _____.

3. _____ _____ an old shirt.

4. _____ sweater is new.

5. _____ car is expensive.

3. Listening task

Listen. Write the names by the pictures.

| Anne | Brenda | Carol | David | Edward | Frank |

Pair Practice A

Student A look at this page. Student B look at page 24.

Language Key

Say	Answer
Picture 1 has one table. There are two white cups.	Yes, I see it. That's Picture E.

You have pictures 1 to 6. Your partner has pictures A to F.
Talk to your partner. Describe the pictures and find the matches.

1.  ❏

2.  ❏

3.  ❏

4.  ❏

5.  ❏

6.  ❏

EXTRA! EXTRA!

Memory Game

Look at the picture for one minute. Then close your book. Can you remember the things in the picture? Your partner will check the picture.

There are two coats.

That's right.

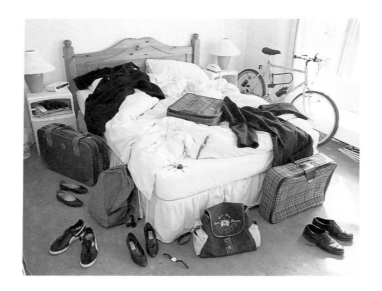

Social Talk—Offering

3

1. Listen in 🖭

Listen to the conversations.

1.

> Here, have some coffee.
> Oh, thank you.

2.
> Would you like a drink?
> Yes, please. Orange juice is fine.

3.
> Would you like a drink?
> No, thanks. Nothing for me.

4.

> Would you like some coffee or tea?
> Tea, please.

2. Act it out

Work in pairs. Practice the conversations.

Pair Practice B

Student B look at this page. Student A look at page 22.

Language Key	
Say	Answer
Picture E has one table. There are two white cups.	Yes, I see it. That's Picture 1.

You have pictures A to F. Your partner has pictures 1 to 6.
Talk to your partner. Describe the pictures and find the matches.

A.  ❑

B.  ❑

C.  ❑

D.  ❑

E.  ❑

F.  ❑

EXTRA! EXTRA!

Memory Game

Look at the picture for one minute. Then close your book. Can you remember the things in the picture? Your partner will check the picture.

There are two coats.

That's right.

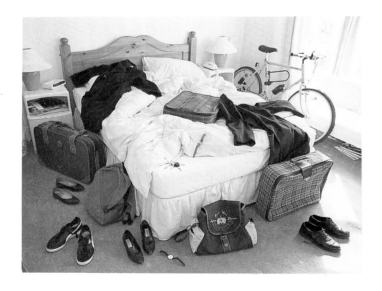

Challenge Unit

1. Conversation Review

Look at Tables 1, 2, and 3. Make short conversations.

Table 1. How are you?

Hello, John.		Fine, thanks. And you?
How are you?		Good.
How are you doing?		Not bad.
How are you today?		OK.
How are you this morning?		Great. How about you?
How are you this evening?		

Table 2. Goodbye.

Goodbye, Ms. Adams.		See you later, Mr. Nakano.
		Dr. Smith.
		Mrs. Choy.
		Tom.
		Susan.
Have a nice weekend.		Thanks.
		Thanks. You too.
		Thanks. Bye!
		Bye. Have a good day.

Table 3. Offers.

Here's some _____.		Oh, thank you.
Would you like some _____?		No, thanks.
Would you like a _____?		_____, please.
Would you like _____ or _____?		

2. Question and Answer Review

Match the answers with the questions.

Answers	Questions
She's Chinese.	How are you today?
Five.	How many books do you have?
It's Mary's.	How old is Mari?
They're Mary's.	Is this your sweater?
Fine, thank you.	What nationality is Sue?
No, it isn't. My sweater is blue.	What's your address?
She's 21.	What's your name?
353-0909.	What's your phone number?
919 Carter Street.	Whose book is this?
Sam Johnson.	Whose keys are these?
No, I don't. But I have a bicycle.	Is your watch new?
No, it isn't. It's old.	Do you have a car?

3. Grammar Watch

Check (✓) the correct sentence. Circle the error.

1.	She Chinese.	She's Chinese.
2.	This book is Mary's.	This book is Mary.
3.	This is Mary book.	This is Mary's book.
4.	Is your watch new?	Your watch new?
5.	Mark is 24 year old.	Mark is 24 years old.
6.	What your favorite movie?	What's your favorite movie?
7.	How old you are?	How old are you?
8.	My books new.	My books are new.
9.	My books are new.	My books is new.
10.	There is a book on my desk.	There are a book on my desk.
11.	He have two books.	He has two books.
12.	We have a new car.	We have new car.

4. Vocabulary Expansion

What's the pattern? Complete these word lists.
Use these words or other words:

(212) 992-3000	brother	messy	thirteen	they're
Tokyo 101 JAPAN	daughter	Mexican	address	wife
aren't	favorite song	Mike	she's	
book	Italian	pants	Tom's	
Brazilian	Mary	small	Korean	

1. Canadian   American   _____   Nicaraguan   Panamanian

2. Columbian   Venezuelan   _____   Argentinean   Chilean

3. German   French   _____   Greek   Swiss

4. Thai   Malaysian   _____   Vietnamese   Cambodian

5. father   mother   _____   sister

6. husband   _____   son   _____

7. I'm   you're   he's   _____   it's   we're   you're   _____

8. is   isn't   are   _____

9. Peter   Alex   _____   Mr. Jackson   Andy

10. Karen   Beth   _____   Ms. Smith   Lisa

11. Mary   Mary's   Tom   _____

12. Los Angeles, California 90011 USA   London W1 ENGLAND
_____

13. (213) 975-6843   _____   (03) 3404-6925

14. favorite movie   favorite book   favorite food   _____

15. name   _____   phone number

16. pen   pencil   paper   _____

17. new   old   large   _____

18. four   seven   ten   _____

19. expensive   cheap   neat   _____

20. shirt   skirt   coat   _____

5. Interaction Game–Favorites

Play this game with three people. Use paper clips or erasers as markers. Flip a coin. Move your marker. Ask the question to the person on your right. A correct answer = one point. When the first player reaches the goal, count the points. Who wins?

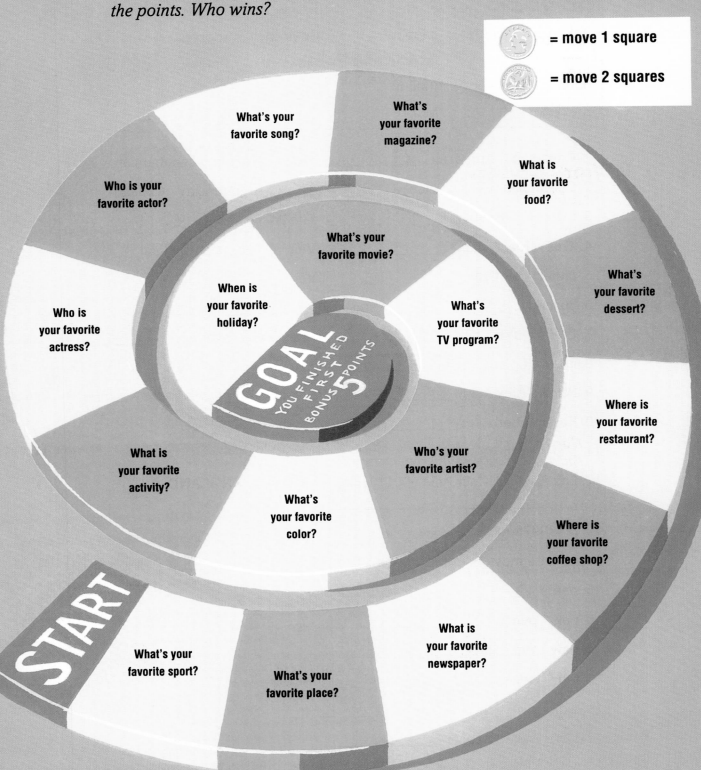

First Try

1. Pronunciation

Listen and repeat.

> Who?   Who's...?   Who's that?   That's my sister.
>
> Is that your brother?   No, it isn't.   That's my husband.
>
> Does she live in the States?   No, she doesn't.   She lives in Japan.

2. Work in pairs

First listen to the conversations. Then practice in pairs.

1.

Who's that?
That's my sister, Lena.

2.

Is that your brother?
No, that's my husband, Tony.

3.

Who's that?
That's my friend, Mike.
Does he live in San Francisco?
Yes, he does.

4.

Who's that?
That's my sister, Ellen.
Does she live in the States?
No, she doesn't. She lives in Japan.

3. Let's try it

Complete these conversations.

1.

Is that your _____?
No, that's my _____,
_____.

2.

Who's that?
That's _____.
Does _____ live in
_____?
No, _____ _____.
_____ *lives in* _____.

Word Bank 📼

Listen and look at the pictures. Then repeat the words.

Lives in Boston, Sydney, Frankfurt

Lives at 101 South First Street

Works at Apple Computer Company

Companies (Places to work)

Works at/Works for:

Harrod's Department Store   University of California

Ritz Hotel   Commodore Publishing Company

Burger Prince   Longview Hospital

Toyota Motor Company   (City, District, Federal) Government

Places to work

an office   a school/university

a clinic

home

a factory

a lab

a store

Occupations

student   teacher

businessperson

(businessman, businesswoman)

salesperson   (salesman, saleswoman)

engineer   parent

doctor   scientist

reporter   actor

Adjectives

busy   quiet   noisy   crowded

1. Does she...?

Ask and answer. Yes, he/she does. *or* No, he/she doesn't.

1.
Does she live in Los Angeles?

2.
Does she live in London?

3.
Does she live in New York?

4.
Does Mr. Park work at Apple Computer Company?

5.
Does he work at IBM?

6.
Does he work at Jefferson High School?

2. ID Card

Make sentences.

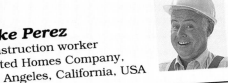

Mike Perez
Construction worker
United Homes Company,
Los Angeles, California, USA

His name is _____.
He's a _____.
He lives in _____.
He works at _____.

Eri Toyama
Doctor
Tokyo Medical Center,
Yokohama, Japan

Her name is _____.
She's a _____.
She lives in _____.
She works at _____.

Sarah Karloff
Sales Representative
Digit Computer Company,
Toronto, Canada

Her name is _____.
She's a _____.
She lives in _____.
She works at _____.

3. How about you?

Ask your partner.

	You	Partner
Where do you live?	_____	_____
What do you do? (What's your job?)	_____	_____
Where do you work/study?	_____	_____
What is the name of your company/school ?	_____	_____

Listening

5

1. **Easy listening** 📼

Listen to each conversation. Make a check (✓) on the correct picture.

Actor ❑

Basketball Player ❑

University of California ❑

Home ❑

Burger Prince ❑

Teacher ❑

Scientist ❑

Student ❑

2. Listening dictation

Listen. Which expression? Check it (✓). Then complete the response.

1. _____ Where does he live?
   _____ Does he live here?   He _____ in Tokyo.

2. _____ What do you do?
   _____ What does she do?   _____ _____ lawyer.

3. _____ Is she a teacher?
   _____ What does she do?   _____, _____ _____.

4. _____ Do they live in Seoul?
   _____ Where do they live?   _____ _____ in Seoul.

5. _____ Are they students?
   _____ Are you students?   _____, _____ _____.

6. _____ Are you American?
   _____ Where are you from?   _____, _____ _____. I'm from California.

3. Listening task

Listen. Complete the information.

Mariah Carey

She lives in _____.
She is a _____.

Michael Jordan

He lives in _____.
He is a _____.

Amy Tan

She lives in _____.
She is a _____.

Oliver Stone

He lives in _____.
He is a _____.

Pair Practice A

Student A look at this page. Student B look at page 36.

Language Key	
Ask	Answer
What does (name) do?	She's a (scientist).
Where does she live?	She lives in (London).

Look at the pictures. Ask questions. Find the missing information. Write the words.

1.

Deion Sanders

_____

Atlanta

2.

Jodie Foster

_____

New York

3.

Whoopi Goldberg

_____

Los Angeles

4.

Gary Larson
Cartoonist

_____

5.

Jeremy Irons
Actor

_____

6.

Yannick Noah
Tennis coach

_____

EXTRA! EXTRA!

Famous People

How many do you know? Check the ones you know. Tell your partner:

Number 1 is _____.

1.

musician ☐

2.

actor ☐

3.

musician ☐

4.

politician ☐

Social Talk—Introductions

1. Listen in

Listen to the conversations.

1.

Hi, Richard.

Hi, Mary. Mary, I'd like you to meet Jesse.

Hi, Jesse. Glad to meet you.

Glad to meet you too, Mary.

2.

Dad, this is Neville.

Oh, hello, Neville. Glad to meet you.

Glad to meet you too, Mr. Simpson.

3.

Hi Marc. Who's your friend?

Oh, let me introduce you. Amy, this is Elena. Elena, Amy.

Nice to meet you, Amy.

Nice to meet you, Elena.

4.

I want to introduce my friend, Paula.

Oh, hello, Paula. Glad to meet you. I'm David.

Hello, David. Glad to meet you too.

2. Act it out

Work in pairs. Practice the conversations.

Pair Practice B 👥

Student B look at this page. Student A look at page 34.

Language Key	
Ask	**Answer**
What does (name) do?	She's a (scientist).
Where does she live?	She lives in (London).

Look at the pictures. Ask questions. Find the missing information. Write the words.

1.

   Deion Sanders
   Baseball player

   _____

2.

   Jodie Foster
   Actress

   _____

3.

   Whoopi Goldberg
   Actress

   _____

4.

   Gary Larson

   _____

   San Francisco

5.

   Jeremy Irons

   _____

   London

6.

   Yannick Noah

   _____

   Paris, France

EXTRA! EXTRA! 👥

Famous People

How many do you know? Check the ones you know. Tell your partner:

Number 1 is _____.

1.

   musician ☐

2.

   actor ☐

3.

   musician ☐

4.

   politician ☐

First Try

1. Pronunciation

Listen and repeat.

> How?   When?   How often?
>
> How's your job?   When do you work?
>
> How often do you drive?   I drive every day.

2. Work in pairs

First listen to the conversations. Then practice in pairs.

1.
How is your new job?
It's OK.
When do you work?
I work from 8 until 5.

2.
How is your new class?
It's not bad.
When do you go to class?
I go to class on Mondays, Wednesdays, and Fridays.

3.
How's your new car?
It's fine.
How often do you drive it?
I drive it every day.

4.
How's your new bicycle?
It's great.
How often do you ride it?
I ride it every weekend.

3. Let's try it

Complete these conversations.

1. How's your _____ _____?
It's _____.
When do _____?
I _____ from _____.

2. How's your _____ _____?
It's _____.
How often do _____?
I _____.

Word Bank

Listen and look at the pictures. Then repeat the words.

Daily activities

get up   eat breakfast   go to work   go home

go shopping   watch television   listen to music   study

do housework   take a bath   take a shower   go to bed

Times

Times of day: in the morning   in the afternoon   in the evening   at night

Days and months

on Monday   on Mondays, Wednesdays, and Fridays   Monday through Friday

on the weekend   every day   every week

in January   January through March   in November and December

Adverbs

always   usually   sometimes   never
100%   50-75%   25%   0%

early   late

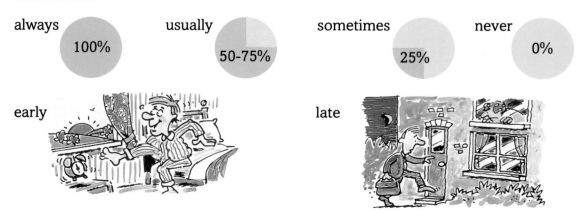

1. What time is it?

Point to the clocks. Ask the time.

What time is it?   It's 2 o'clock. *or* It's about 2 o'clock.

| 2:00 | 2:30 | 2:55 | 4:15 | 6:00 | 9:25 |

2. What time?

Ask and answer.

What time do you (get up)?   *I (get up) at 7 o'clock.*
or I usually (get up) at 7 o'clock.

	You	Your partner	Who is later?
get up	_____	_____	_____
eat breakfast	_____	_____	_____
eat lunch	_____	_____	_____
go to bed	_____	_____	_____

3. How often?

How often do you...? Ask and answer.

100% always	75% usually	25–50% often	10–25% sometimes	5–10% hardly ever	0% never

get up at 5:00 a.m.
drink coffee in the morning
watch TV in the evening
eat dinner at home
eat lunch at a fast food restaurant

go to rock concerts on the weekend
listen to music during dinner
go to work by train
ski in January
swim in July

New Words

Do you know more words?

Daily activities _____

Listening

1. Easy listening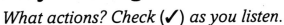

What actions? Check (✓) as you listen.

[Row of illustrated pictures with checkboxes below each]

❏   ❏   ❏

❏   ❏   ❏

❏   ❏   ❏

2. Listening dictation 🔲

Listen. Write the times.

Andy gets up at _____.

He leaves home at _____.

He gets to work at _____.

He eats lunch at _____.

He leaves work at _____.

He gets home at _____.

What's next? First write the words. Then listen. Check your answers.

1. When _____ _____ get up? *I* _____ _____ _____ *at 9:00.*

2. _____ do you _____ lunch? *I always* _____ _____ *at 1:00.*

3. _____ _____ you get home? *I* _____ _____ *at 6:30.*

3. Listening task 📼

Put the pictures in order. Write 1 to 6.

Pair Practice A 👥

Student A look at this page. Student B look at page 44.

Language Key	
Ask	Answer
What time does she (eat dinner)?	At 6 o'clock.
When does she (go home)?	

Marla Mitchell is an executive for Angelica Records. Ask your partner about her schedule. Write the missing information and put the pictures in order 1 to 6.

drive to work
time: _____

go jogging
time: _____

have a meeting
time: _____

go to a concert
time: _____

get dressed
time: _____

make dinner
time: _____

Now listen to your partner's questions about Tim Rourke's schedule. Give short answers.

Tim Rourke	
get dressed 6:30	go to a dinner 5:00
make breakfast 7:00	give a speech 6:00
write letters 10:30	watch TV 10:00

• •

EXTRA! EXTRA! 👥

Do you... every day?

What do you do every day? Ask your partner.

Do you (read a newspaper) every day?
Yes, I do. or *No, I don't.* or *Sometimes, but not every day.*

Social Talk—Excuse me

6

1. Listen in 📼

Listen to the conversations.

1.
> Excuse me. Is this the Video Room?
>
> Yes, that's right.

2.
> Wait! That's the women's room.
>
> Oh, really?
>
> Yes, the men's room is over there.
>
> Oh, thanks.

3.
> Excuse me. Where's the train station?
>
> It's over there.
>
> Oh, thanks.

4.
> Excuse me. Is this Michael Jackson's room?
>
> I'm sorry. I don't know.
>
> Thanks, anyway.
>
> You're welcome.

2. Act it out

Work in pairs. Practice the conversations.

Pair Practice B 👥

Student B look at this page. Student A look at page 42.

Student A look at page 42.

Language Key

Ask	Answer
What time does she (eat dinner)?	At 6 o'clock.
When does she (go home)?	

Listen to your partner's questions about Marla Mitchell's schedule. Give short answers.

Marla Mitchell
go jogging 6:30 a.m.	make dinner 5:00
drive to work 8:00	get dressed 6:30
have a meeting 3:00	go to a concert 7:30

Tim Rourke is a politician. Ask your partner about his schedule. Write the missing information and put the pictures in order 1 to 6.

give a speech
time: _____

get dressed
time: _____

make breakfast
time: _____

write letters
time: _____

go to a dinner
time: _____

watch TV
time: _____

• •

EXTRA! EXTRA! 👥

Do you... every day?

What do you do every day? Ask your partner.

Do you (read a newspaper) every day?
Yes, I do. or *No, I don't.* or *Sometimes, but not every day.*

First Try

1. Pronunciation

Listen and repeat.

> Where's...? Is there...? Where is Dr. Jones? She's in her office.
>
> Is there a bank near here? Yes, there is. It's over there. Oh, yes. I see it.

2. Work in pairs

First listen to the conversations. Then practice in pairs.

1.

Is Dr. Jones here?
Yes, she is. She's in her office.
Thank you.

2.

Is there a bank near here?
Yes, there's a bank over there.
Oh, yes. I see it. Thanks.

3.

Where is Todd?
He's between Mark and Laura.
Oh, yes. I see him.

4:

Where's the newspaper?
It's on your desk.
Oh, yes. I see it. Thanks.

3. Let's try it

Complete these conversations.

1.

Is there a _____ near here?
*Yes, there's a _____ next
to _____.*
That's great. Thanks.

2.

Where's _____.
_____'s _____ _____.
Oh, yes. I see _____.

Word Bank 📼

Listen and look at the pictures. Then repeat the words.

Locations

next to
behind
between ... and
under
in
in front of
on
in the corner
on the right side (of)
on the left side (of)

Things in a house

1. newspaper
2. plant
3. letter
4. picture
5. CD player
6. couch
7. camera
8. toy
9. guitar

1. Is there? Are there?

Look at the picture on page 46. Ask and answer.

Is there a.... ?   *Yes, there is. / No, there isn't.*

Put a check (✓) for Yes and a cross (✗) for No.

1. Is there a CD player under the television? ❑
2. Is there a chair near the desk? ❑
3. Is there a newspaper near the television? ❑
4. Are there two plants in the living room? ❑
5. Is there a computer on the desk ? ❑
6. Is the telephone between the computer and the picture? ❑

Ask a partner five more questions about the picture. Answer Yes or No.

2. What is it?

Look at the picture on page 46 again. In pairs, ask and answer.

It's behind the computer. What is it?   *A book.   That's right.*

1. They're on top of the desk.   _____
2. It is in front of the television.   _____
3. It is to the left of the television.   _____
4. It's between the telephone and the computer.   _____
5. They're under the desk.   _____

Ask two more questions.

3. In your classroom?

Ask your partner about the classroom. Write the answers.

Is there a teacher in this room?   *Yes.*
Where is she (or he)?   *Next to the door.*

	Yes or No?	**Where?**
a computer	_____	_____
a newspaper	_____	_____
a backpack	_____	_____
a plant	_____	_____

Ask three more questions.

New Words

Do you know more words?

Things in a room.

_____

7

Listening

1. Easy listening 🔲

Look at the picture. Listen. Put a check (✔) for Yes and a cross (✗) for No.

1. ❑   2. ❑   3. ❑   4. ❑   5. ❑   6. ❑   7. ❑

2. Listening dictation 🔲

Listen. Write the words.

1. _____the newspaper? *It's _____ the table.*

2. _____the computer? *It's _____ _____ the desk.*

3. _____ _____ my shoes? _____ _____ *the bed.*

4. _____ my red sweater? _____ _____ _____.

5. Where is the newspaper? *I don't know. Maybe it's _____ _____ _____.*

3. **Listening task**

Draw lines from the names to the people in the picture.

Andy **Mike** **Meilin** **Tracy** **Rosanne** **Ben**

Pair Practice A 👥

Student A look at this page. Student B look at page 52.

Language Key	
Ask	Answer
Is there (a man with a hat) in your picture?	Yes, there is. *or* No, there isn't.
Where is he?	He's next to ...
Are there (two girls)?	Yes, there are. *or* No, there aren't.

Look at your picture. B has a different picture.

Ask questions. Find the differences and circle them.

Ask about: a man with a beard   a woman with a white hat

a man with a striped jacket   a woman in a striped dress   two girls

EXTRA! EXTRA! 👥

Three Changes

Look at your partner's desk. Then close your eyes. Your partner changes three things. Find the three changes.

Now the pencil is under the book.   *Right. That's one change.*

Social Talk—Favors

1. Listen in

Listen to the conversations.

1.

Mary, here's your mail.

Thanks.

You're welcome.

2.

Could you give me a hand?

Sure.

Thanks a lot.

No problem.

3.

What's the matter?

I can't open the door.

Here, let me do it.

Thanks.

4.

Martin, can you do me a favor?

Sure. What is it?

Please mail this for me.

OK, I'd be glad to.

2. Act it out

Work in pairs. Practice the conversations.

Pair Practice B

Student B look at this page. Student A look at page 50.

Language Key

Ask	Answer
Is there a (man with a hat) in your picture?	Yes, there is. *or* No, there isn't.
Where is he?	He's next to ...
Are there (two girls)?	Yes, there are. *or* No, there aren't.

Look at your picture. A has a different picture.
Ask questions. Find the differences and circle them.
Ask about: a man with a beard   a woman with a white hat
a man with a striped jacket   a woman in a striped dress   two girls

EXTRA! EXTRA!

Three Changes
Look at your partner's desk. Then close your eyes. Your partner changes three things. Find the three changes.

Now the pencil is under the book.   *Right. That's one change.*

Challenge Unit

1. Question and Answer Review

Match the answers with the questions.

Answers	Questions
Every day.	Does she live in Toronto?
I wash the dishes.	How many books are there?
In New York.	How often do you ride the bus?
It's OK. I like it.	How's your new job?
It's on the desk.	Is she a doctor?
No, she doesn't.	Is there a newspaper on the table?
No, thank you.	What do you do after dinner?
On Monday.	What does your sister do?
She's an accountant.	When do you go to class?
There are two.	Where do they live?
Yes, she is.	Where's the newspaper?
Yes, there is.	Would you like a drink?

2. Grammar Watch

Check (✓) the correct sentence. Circle the error.

1. Who that?   Who's that?
2. Do she live in the States?   Does she live in the States?
3. That my husband.   That's my husband.
4. He works Apple Computer Company.   He works at Apple Computer Company.
5. What does she do?   What she do?
6. She's doctor.   She's a doctor.
7. They live Seoul.   They live in Seoul.
8. He gets up 7:00.   He gets up at 7:00.

3. Vocabulary Game–Word Images

Divide into two teams.
One member from Team A picks a word or phrase.
He or she draws a picture on the board.
Can Team A guess the word or phrase?
There is a 15 second time limit.
A correct guess = 1– 4 points.
Then Team B tries.
The first team with 10 points wins the game.

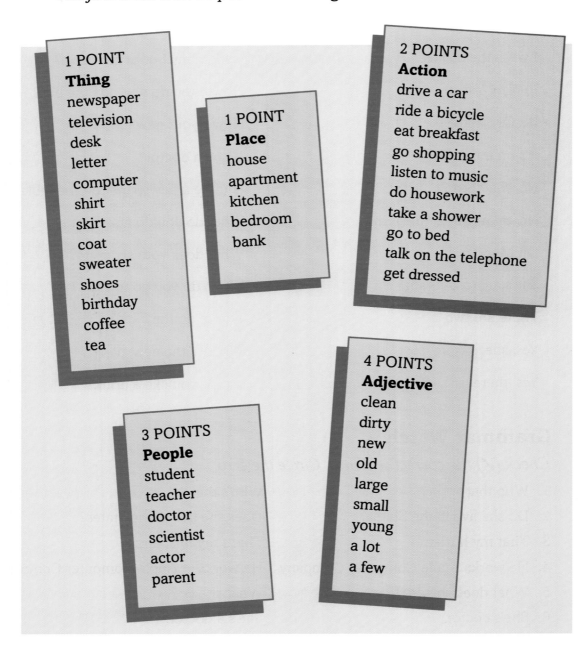

1 POINT
Thing
newspaper
television
desk
letter
computer
shirt
skirt
coat
sweater
shoes
birthday
coffee
tea

1 POINT
Place
house
apartment
kitchen
bedroom
bank

2 POINTS
Action
drive a car
ride a bicycle
eat breakfast
go shopping
listen to music
do housework
take a shower
go to bed
talk on the telephone
get dressed

4 POINTS
Adjective
clean
dirty
new
old
large
small
young
a lot
a few

3 POINTS
People
student
teacher
doctor
scientist
actor
parent

4. Language Game–Guess what?

Play in a group of four. Take turns. One person thinks of something in the room. Others guess. How many guesses?

I'm thinking of something in this room and it's (green).

Clues

color (It's green.)
place (It's in front of Tom.)
adjective (It's big.)

Guesses

① ② ③ ④

What was it?

_____

5. Language Game–Maps

Is there a....?

Work in groups of four. Look at the map. Choose a place.
Ask, "Is there a (bank) near here?" Find the place on the map.
Then say, "Yes, there is. It's on (First Street)."

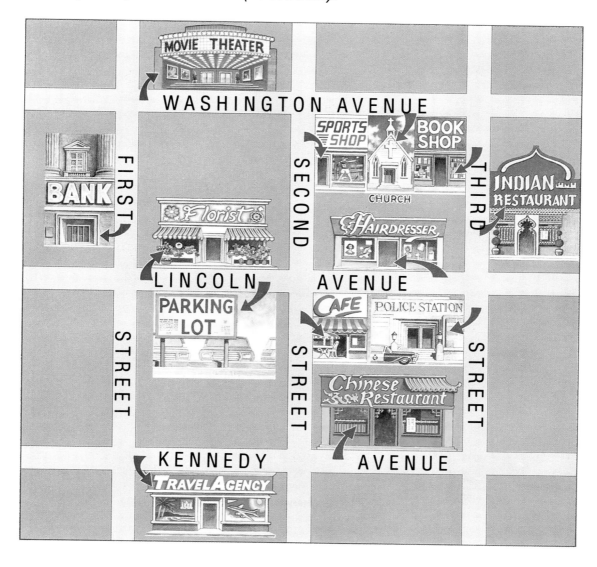

5. Interaction Game—Personal Information

Play this game with four people.
Use paperclips or erasers as markers.
Each person starts at a different corner.
Flip a coin. Move your marker.
Ask the question to the person on your right.
A correct answer = one point.
When the first player reaches the goal, count the points. Who wins?

= move 1 square

= move 2 squares

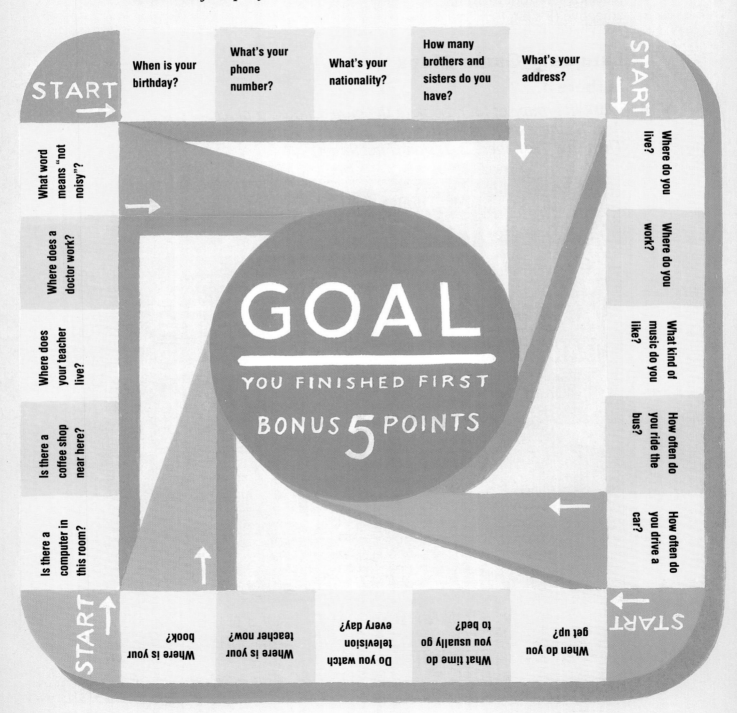

First Try

1. Pronunciation

Listen and repeat.

> Where are...? What's he...? Is Mr. Maxwell in his office?
>
> What's he doing? Where are they? What are they doing?
>
> They're in the yard. They're playing soccer.

2. Work in pairs

First listen to the conversations. Then practice in pairs.

1.

Is Mr. Maxwell in the office?
No, he's in the cafeteria.
He's eating lunch.

2.

Are Tim and Charlie in the
classroom?
No, they aren't. They're in the library.
They're studying.

3.

Where's Maria?
She's in the living room.
What's she doing?
She's reading the newspaper.

4.

Where are Bob and Sally?
They're in the yard.
What are they doing?
They're playing soccer.

3. Let's try it

Complete these conversations.

1.

Where's _____?
He's / She's in _____.
What's he/she doing?
_____.

2.

Where are _____ and
_____?
They're in _____.
What are they doing?
_____.

Word Bank 📼

Listen and look at the pictures. Then repeat the words.

Activities at home

washing the dishes

relaxing

playing baseball

sleeping

talking on the telephone

doing homework

fixing a car

cooking

exercising

riding a bicycle

cleaning the house

reading the newspaper

Adjectives

easy

difficult

interesting

boring

1. Do you like it?

Ask and answer in pairs. Say each activity.

Do you like (cooking)?
Answer:

I love it!	I really like it.	I like it.	I like it a little.	I don't like it.	I hate it!

cooking   cleaning   exercising   eating   drinking beer   going on dates
going to the movies   going to weddings   driving fast cars
listening to rap music   watching Walt Disney movies

2. Word puzzle

Ask and answer in pairs.

What is Number 1?	*I think it's "Talk on the telephone."*
How do you spell telephone?	*T-E-L-E-P-H-O-N-E.*

1. Talk on the _ _ _ _ _ _ _ _ _

2. Play _ _ _ _ _ _ _ _

3. Fix a _ _ _

4. Wash the _ _ _ _ _ _

5. Do _ _ _ _ _ _ _ _

6. Ride a _ _ _ _ _ _ _

3. Actions

Choose an action. Act.
Your partner will guess.

Actions

drink coffee	get up	get washed
eat a sandwich	play soccer	relax on the
wash dishes	sleep	sofa
study English	get dressed	talk on the
read a	watch television	telephone
newspaper	do housework	cook dinner

Think of three more actions.

What am I doing?

You're cooking?

New Words

Write down new words to learn here.

Actions

_____

Listening

9

1. Easy listening

Listen. Match the pictures. Write the numbers in the correct boxes.

1. He's hungry

2. She's thirsty.

3. Her tape player is broken.

4. The dishes are dirty.

5. The coffee is ready.

6. He's very tired.

7. She's very tired.

8. She's hungry.

2. Listening dictation

Listen. Choose the answer and circle it.

1. a. Yes, he is.
   b. He's in the kitchen.

2. a. Yes, she is.
   b. Yes, he is.

3. a. Yes, she is.
   b. Yes, they are.

4. a. I'm in the living room.
   b. He's in the living room.

5. a. They're eating dinner.
   b. We're eating dinner.

6. a. No, I'm not.
   b. You're in the kitchen.

Listen. Write the words.

1. _____ Mr. Rainer in the office?
   Yes, _____ _____.
   _____ _____ _____ a report?
   No, he isn't. _____ talking on the telephone.

2. _____ Lara ____ ____ _____?
   No, she isn't.
   _____ _____ _____?
   She's in the garage.
   _____ she _____?
   She's fixing the car.

3. Listening Task

Draw a line from each name to the picture.

Mr. Adams

Ms. Green, Mr. Andersen and Ms. Becker

Mr. Buford

Mr. Allen and Ms. Perkins

Mr. Martinez and Ms. Dawkins

Mr. Ivy and Ms. Quinn

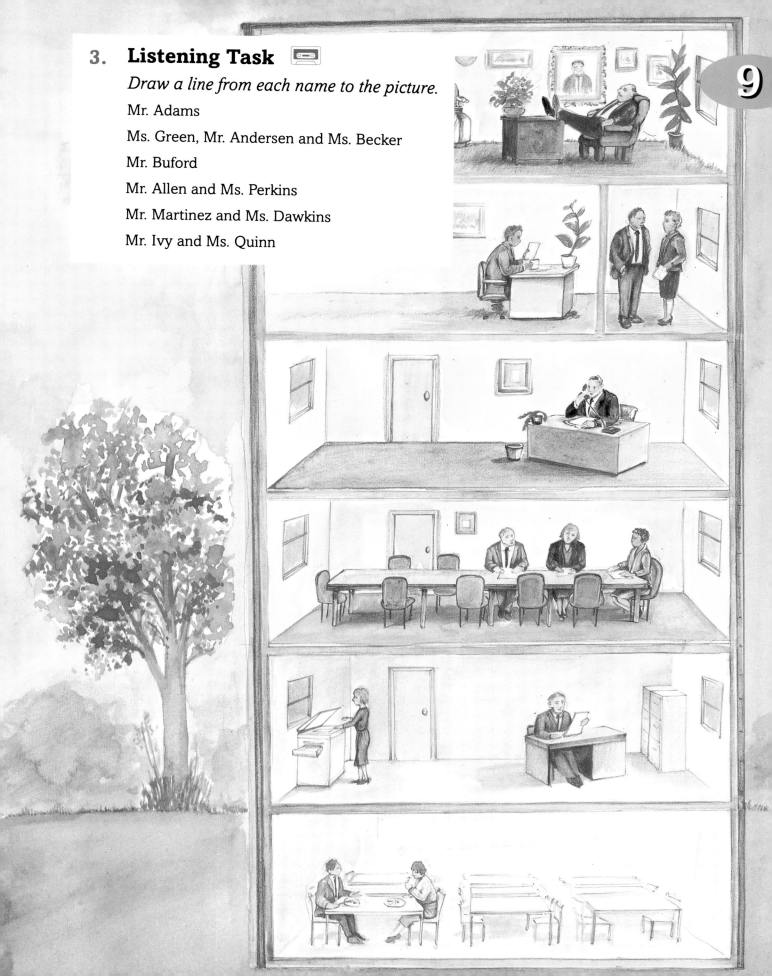

Pair Practice A

Student A look at this page. Student B look at page 64.

Language Key

Ask	Answer
What is she doing?	She's (eating dinner).
What are they doing?	They're (watching television).

Look at pictures 5, 6, 7 and 8. Ask your partner: What are they doing?
Answer your partner's questions about pictures 1, 2, 3 and 4.

1. He's a businessman. He's talking on the telephone.

2. He's a musician. He's playing the piano.

3. She's a doctor. She's talking to a patient.

4. She's a chef. She's cooking something.

5. They're singers.
_____
_____

6. They're soccer players.
_____
_____

7. She's a secretary.
_____
_____

8. She's an artist.
_____
_____

EXTRA! EXTRA!

Three Questions

Think of a person. Your partner asks three questions and then guesses who.

Is it a woman? Is she next to the door? Is she wearing a red sweater? Is it Naomi?

Social Talk—Requests

9

1. Listen in 📼

Listen to the conversations.

1.
> The door's open. Can you close it?
> Sure.

2.
> The music's too loud. Please turn it down.
> OK. Sorry.

3.
> Shall I open the window?
> No, please don't. I'm cold.

4.
> No, please don't do that!
> Why not?
> It's dangerous!

2. Act it out

Work in pairs. Practice the conversations.

Pair Practice B

Student B look at this page. Student A look at page 62.

Language Key

Ask	Answer
What is she doing?	She's (eating dinner).
What are they doing?	They're (watching television).

Look at pictures 1, 2, 3 and 4. Ask your partner: What are they doing?
Answer your partner's questions about pictures 5, 6, 7 and 8.

1. He's a businessman.
   _____
   _____

2. He's a musician.
   _____
   _____

3. She's a doctor.
   _____
   _____

4. She's a chef.
   _____
   _____

5. They're singers.
   They're singing a
   song.

6. They're soccer
   players. They're
   playing a match.

7. She's a secretary.
   She's typing a
   report.

8. She's an artist.
   She's painting a
   picture.

• •

EXTRA! EXTRA!

Three Questions

Think of a person. Your partner asks three questions and then guesses who.

Is it a woman? Is she next to the door? Is she wearing a red sweater? Is it Naomi?

UNIT TEN

First Try

1. Pronunciation

Listen and repeat.

> any apples   Do we need any apples?   Don't
>
> Don't buy any.   How many?   How many do we need?
>
> How much?   How much would you like?

2. Work in pairs

First listen to the conversations. Then practice in pairs.

1.

Do we need any apples?
Yes, we do. Please get six.
Sure.

2.

Do we need any bread?
No, we don't. Don't buy any.

3.

Do you have any rice?
Yes. How much would you like?
2 kilos please.
Sure. Here you are.

4.

Do we need any orange juice?
Yes.
How many cans do we need?
Four cans.

3. Let's try it

Complete these conversations.

1.

Do we need any _____s ?
Yes, we do. Please get _____.
Sure.

2.

Do we need any _____?
Yes.
How _____ do we need?
Please get _____.

Word Bank

Listen and look at the pictures. Then repeat the words.

Food

Some   rice   milk   butter   cheese

Some   cookies   onions   apples   grapes   eggs

One   cookie   onion   apple   grape   egg

How much?   rice   cheese   milk

How many?   grapes   oranges   apples

How much/How many?

 two cans of soup   one loaf of bread   a carton of eggs   three bottles of wine

Singular (1)
1 kilo of beef   1 liter of milk
1 kilo of chicken   1 liter of juice

Plural (more than 1)
2 kilos of beef   2 liters of milk
2 kilos of chicken   2 liters of juice

Containers

a bag of rice   two bags of rice
a bottle of ketchup, soy sauce, wine   two bottles of ketchup
a can of beer   two cans of beer
a carton of milk   two cartons of milk

Some adjectives

hot   cold   delicious   juicy

round   square

1. Do we have any...?

Ask and answer. Do we have any ...?

> Do we have any grapes?
> Yes, we have some. / No, we don't have any.

1. butter
2. oranges
3. cookies
4. cheese
5. grapes
6. onions
7. ketchup
8. wine
9. rice
10. milk

2. How much/how many?

Look at the pictures above. Ask and answer.

> How much _____ do we have? *or*
> How many _____s do we have?

1. rice   2. cookies   3. onions   4. milk   5. wine

3. Shopping list

Ask and answer.

> How many (eggs) do we need?   *We need two cartons.*
>
> How many (kilos of rice)
> How much (rice) } do we need?   *We need 5 kilos.*

List
eggs
butter
wine
cheese
rice
cookies
grapes

New Words

Do you know any more foods? _____

Listening

1. Easy listening

Where is it? Draw a line to the correct place.

cereal

potato chips

cooking oil

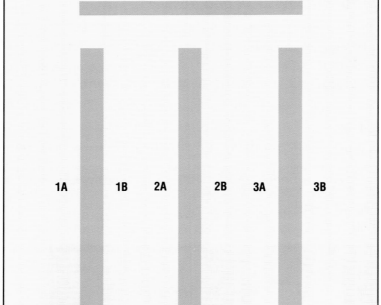

flowers

soap

ice cream

pasta

fish

carts

2. Listening dictation

Listen and write the words.

1. We need _____ _____ _____ cheese.

2. Please buy ___ _____ ____ cola.

3. They need _____ cartons _____ orange juice.

4. Could I have _____ _____ of coffee, please?

5. I'd like _____ bottles of wine.

6. How _____ apples do we _____?

7. Do we _____ _____ _____?

8. How _____ butter should I buy?

3. Listening task

Listen. Complete this shopping list.

_____ milk

_____ eggs

_____ rice

_____ bread

_____ oranges

_____ apples

_____ potato chips

_____ soda

UNIT TEN

Pair Practice A 👥

Student A look at this page. Student B look at page 72.

Language Key

Ask		Answer
Do we need any ....?		Yes, we need some.
How many do we have?	How much do we have?	No, we don't need any.
How many do we need?	How much do we need?	We should buy ....
How many should we buy?	How much should we buy?	

Look at the shopping list. Ask your partner:
How many do we have? How many do we need?
Complete the shopping list.

We have	We need	Please buy
3 oranges	15 oranges	12 oranges
no orange juice	_____	_____
1 bottle of soy sauce	_____	_____
_____	6 cans of soda	_____
1 kilo of rice	_____	_____
1 loaf of bread	_____	_____
no bags of cookies	_____	_____
_____	300 grams of coffee	_____
_____	1 kilo of cheese	_____
1 liter of milk	_____	

• •

EXTRA! EXTRA! 👥

Shopping Trip

What did you buy last week? Tell your partner.
Write your partner's list.

I bought (a shirt and some magazines and ...).

Social Talk—Shopping

1. Listen in

Listen to the conversations.

1.

2.

3.

4.

2. Act it out

Work in pairs. Practice the conversations.

Pair Practice B 👥

Student B look at this page. Student A look at page 70.

Language Key

Ask		Answer
Do we need any ....?		Yes, we need some.
How many do we have?	How much do we have?	No, we don't need any.
How many do we need?	How much do we need?	We should buy ....
How many should we buy?	How much should we buy?	

Look at the shopping list. Ask your partner:
How many do we have? How many do we need?
Complete the shopping list.

We have	We need	Please buy
3 oranges	15 oranges	12 oranges
_____	1 liter of orange juice	_____
_____	2 bottles of soy sauce	_____
no cans of soda	_____	_____
_____	3 kilos of rice	_____
_____	2 loaves of bread	_____
_____	1 bag of cookies	_____
100 grams of coffee	_____	_____
½ kilo of cheese	_____	_____
_____	3 liters of milk	_____

• •

EXTRA! EXTRA! 👥

Shopping Trip

What did you buy last week? Tell your partner.
Write your partner's list.

I bought (a shirt and some magazines and ...).

First Try

1. Pronunciation

Listen and repeat.

> yesterday   do   did you   What did you do yesterday?
>
> where   where were you   Where were you yesterday?
>
> visit   visited   I visited the president.

2. Work in pairs

First listen to the conversations. Then practice in pairs.

1.

Where were you yesterday?
I was at the hospital.
What did you do there?
I visited my father.

2.

Where were you last Sunday?
I was at my sister's house.
What did you do there?
I watched television.

3.

Where were you yesterday?
I was in Washington.
Who did you visit?
I visited the President.

4.

Where were you last Saturday?
I was at the shopping mall.
What did you buy?
I bought some new clothes.

3. Let's try it

1.

Where were you _____?
I was _____.
What did you _____?
_____.

2.

Where were you _____?
I was _____.
What did you _____?
_____.

Word Bank 📼

Listen and look at the pictures. Then repeat the words.

Past actions

is/are—was/were	buy—bought	go—went	listen—listened
has/have—had	eat—ate	watch—watched	visit—visited
do/does—did	meet—met	cook—cooked	

got a letter

went on a holiday

won a prize

saw a movie

took a walk in
the country

did my homework

read the newspaper

wrote a letter

bought a new car

Time expressions

on Friday night   one hour ago   last night   yesterday   last week   last month

last year   in 1990   two years ago

1. Yes, I did.

Ask and answer.

> Did you (eat pizza) last night?   *Yes, I did.* or *No, I didn't.*

go to a restaurant   cook dinner   visit a friend
eat pizza   listen to some good music do your English homework
watch a good TV program   buy a newspaper   sleep well

Ask three more questions.

2. Imagination

Say and ask. Use your imagination.

1. I went somewhere.   Where did you go?   I went to _____.
2. I bought something.   What did you buy?   I bought a _____.
3. I cooked something.   What did you _____?   I cooked a _____.
4. I visited someone.   Who did you _____?   _____.
5. I watched something.   What did you _____?   _____.
6. I listened to something. What did you _____?   _____.
7. I ate something.   What did you _____?   _____.
8. I learned something.   What did you _____?   _____.

3. New words

How many of these actions do you know? What is the present tense?

answered _____   got _____   saw _____
brought _____   knew _____   swam _____
came _____   learned _____   thought _____
caught _____   left _____   took _____
changed _____   lost _____   understood _____
closed _____   loved _____   walked _____
drank _____   made _____   went _____
drove _____   opened _____   won _____
finished _____   played _____   wore _____
flew _____   read _____   wrote _____
gave _____   sang _____   worked _____

Listening

1. Easy listening

Check (✓) the actions that you hear.

❑   ❑   ❑

❑   ❑   ❑

2. Listening dictation

Listen and write the words.

1. go to the beach   – I _____ to the beach yesterday.

2. have a meeting   – We _____ a meeting yesterday.

3. pass my English test – I _____ my English test.

4. like my report   – He _____ my report.

5. buy some tickets   – We _____ some tickets for the game.

6. go to a movie   – _____ you _____ _____ _____ _____ last night?

7. pass the test   – _____ _____ _____ the test _____ _____?

8. buy some tickets   – _____ _____ _____ _____ _____ for the concert?

3. Listening task 📼

Listen to Roger. What did he do last week? Draw lines from the pictures to the correct days.

Monday   Tuesday   Wednesday   Thursday   Friday   Saturday

Pair Practice A

Student A look at this page. Student B look at page 80.

Language Key

Ask	Say
What did Jenny do on Friday night?	She went to a restaurant.
Who did she go with?	She went with her friend, Alan.
What was the name of the restaurant?	
Where was the restaurant?	

What did they do? Where did they go? Who did they go with? Ask your partner. Write the information.

Penny Stone
She went to a concert on Saturday night.
She went with _____.
The concert was at _____.

Adam Park
He _____ on Sunday.
He went with his sister, Erin.
The name of the park was _____.

Connie Chen
She watched a video on Saturday night.
She was with her husband, Barry.
The title of the movie was _____.

EXTRA! EXTRA!

Past Actions
Find three things that both you and your partner did last week.

Did you (eat a hamburger)?   *Yes, I did.* or *No, I didn't.*

Social Talk—News

1. Listen in

Listen to the conversations.

1.

I passed my test!

That's great. Congratulations!

2.

What's wrong?

I don't feel well.

I'm sorry to hear that.

3.

Guess what? Mary's getting married next week!

Is she really? That's interesting.

4.

How was the party?

Really nice. We had a good time.

Oh, that's good. I'm glad to hear that.

2. Act it out

Work in pairs. Practice the conversations.

Pair Practice B

Student B look at this page. Student A look at page 78.

Language Key	
Ask	Say
What did Jenny do on Friday night?	She went to a restaurant.
Who did she go with?	She went with her friend, Alan.
What was the name of the restaurant?	
Where was the restaurant?	

What did they do? Where did they go? Who did they go with? Ask your partner. Write the information.

Penny Stone
She went to a _____ on Saturday night.
She went with her friend, Carla.
The concert was at the Washington Center.

Adam Park
He went hiking on Sunday.
He went with _____.
The name of the park was "Mountain View Park".

Connie Chen
She _____ on Saturday night.
She was with _____.
The title of the movie was "Batman Returns".

• •

EXTRA! EXTRA!

Past Actions
Find three things that both you and your partner did last week.

| Did you (eat a hamburger)? | *Yes, I did.* or *No, I didn't.* |

Challenge Unit

1. Question and Answer Review

Match the answers with the questions.

Answers	Questions
To the museum.	Do we need any apples?
Yes, we do.	How much rice do we have?
In the kitchen.	How many bananas should I buy?
We have 1 kilo.	How much meat should I buy?
He's cleaning the garage.	What is he doing now?
On the desk.	Where are they?
Yes, I did.	Why is he eating a sandwich?
Please buy 3.	Where is my newspaper?
Because he's hungry.	What did you buy?
Some new shoes.	Where did you go?
Please buy 2 kilos.	Did you drive your car?

2. Grammar Watch

Check (✓) the correct sentence. Circle the error.

1. Is he in office?   Is he in the office?
2. What they are doing?   What are they doing?
3. They're playing soccer.   They playing soccer.
4. We hungry.   We're hungry.
5. He's musician.   He's a musician.
6. She's wearing a red dress now.   She wears a red dress now.
7. Do you have any rices?   Do you have any rice?
8. How many rice do we need?   How much rice do we need?
9. Did you go to school yesterday? Did you went to school yesterday?
10. What did you buy?   What you bought?

3. Vocabulary Game—Containers

Put each item in the correct list.

beans flour mustard cereal honey orange juice cola ice cream
potato chips cookies jam rice cooking oil ketchup soup dish soap
laundry soap soy sauce eggs mayonnaise yogurt milk

CAN

CARTON

JAR

BOTTLE

BAG

BOX

4. Vocabulary Game—What's the word? 👥👥

This is a guessing game. Play in a group of six or more. Choose a card. Act out the word or phrase or draw it. Others guess the word or phrase on the card.

NOUNS	VERBS
sister	live
husband	work
wife	get up
brother	go shopping
doctor	listen to music
parent	eat breakfast
teacher	go to work
student	watch television
office	study
store	go to bed
basketball player	do housework
actor	
businessperson	
movie director	
newspaper	
breakfast	

5. Interaction Game—Responses

Play this game with four people. Use paperclips or erasers as markers.
Flip a coin. Move your marker. Read the question or say the expression.
The person on your right must answer or respond. A correct response = one
point. When the first player reaches the goal, add the points. Who wins?

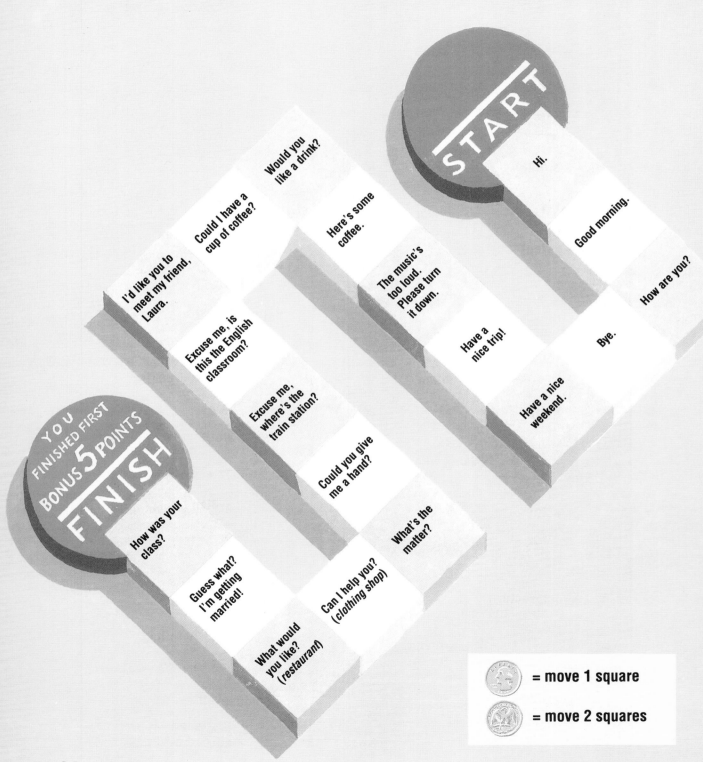

START

Hi.

Good morning.

How are you?

The music's too loud. Please turn it down.

Have a nice trip!

Bye.

Here's some coffee.

Have a nice weekend.

Would you like a drink?

Could I have a cup of coffee?

Excuse me, is this the English classroom?

I'd like you to meet my friend, Laura.

Excuse me, where's the train station?

Could you give me a hand?

What's the matter?

YOU FINISHED FIRST BONUS 5 POINTS FINISH

How was your class?

Guess what? I'm getting married!

Can I help you? (*clothing shop*)

What would you like? (*restaurant*)

= move 1 square

= move 2 squares

12

Classroom Notes

These Classroom Notes will help the teacher make the classroom more active and more communicative, and make the students' learning more enjoyable and more effective. For a more complete teaching guide, please consult the Teacher's Manual.

These notes are divided into two sections: Teaching Procedures and Unit Notes.

Teaching Procedures

Each section in *Real Time English* is designed for 30–60 minutes of classroom work. For most classes, each unit will require about three hours of class time.

First Try

1. Pronunciation Practice

Model the phrases or play the tape. Have the students repeat the phrases, first chorally, then individually. Pay attention especially to stress and intonation.

2. Modeling the Dialogues

Say the lines in the four presentation conversations, or use the tape.
Have the students follow along in their books, or, if they are able, without looking in their books.

3. Class Practice

The students work in pairs. One student is the first speaker in each dialogue; the other student is the second speaker in the dialogue. The students should face each other and make eye contact as they practice. After finishing the dialogues, the students change roles.

4. Acting

The students create their own dialogues, based on the patterns and illustration given, and present them in front of the class. This brief "acting" exercise helps students to internalize the forms they have practiced. It will also help you check student performance.

Word Bank

1. Presentation

Play the tape in which the narrator pronounces the words in short phrases and sentences, or "narrate" the pictures and words yourself. Say the words in the picture as the students point to the pictures and repeat the words. The purpose of this step is to insure general comprehension of the word meanings.

2. Repetition

Ask your students to repeat key words. Ask questions about the picture. (You may wish to have an enlarged photocopy of the page for this purpose.)

3. Active practice

The Word Bank exercises, on the facing page, require the students to process the words actively. Different exercises call for different groupings. Most can be done in pairs, as this will encourage maximum oral work. Demonstrate the first one or two items in each exercise and then allow the students ample time to complete the exercise before checking it.

4. New Words

Students should select words that are new to them and write them down in the New Words box. Ask each student to write down five (or more) new words—words he or she individually would like to learn and remember. You may also ask students to write out illustrative sentences or use some other memory aid. You may also elicit questions from the students about related words that are not on the Word Bank page that they would like to learn.

Also encourage your students to keep Vocabulary Cards. On each card they should write one new word. They should study these regularly and set goals for their own vocabulary learning—such as learning ten new words per week.

Easy Listening

1. Presentation

Play the tape two or three times, or until nearly all of the students can discriminate between the forms (that is, can get the answers correct).

2. Checking

Check the answers. To check the answers, you can simply call out the correct answers orally (1 - b; 2 - a, etc.). Once all the students have checked their answers, replay the taped exercise so that the students can confirm the correct answers. This can be a very useful form of feedback.

Listening Dictation

1. Preview

Read the sentence frames aloud as the students follow along. Say *blank* for each missing word. Ask the students to think about what is missing. This preview will help the students anticipate the correct words. Anticipation is a key process in aural comprehension.

2. Listening and Writing

Play the tape or read the sentences from the Tapescript. Pause after each sentence while the students write. Repeat the sentence if most students have not heard accurately.

3. Check Up

Have the students write the full correct sentence on the board. You may do this after every two sentences, or wait until the students have completed all of the items. Have the students check their own books, circling any items that they have missed. Play the tape a final time so that everyone can check the correct answers.

Listening Task

1. Warm Up

Look at the illustration with the students. Ask questions about the picture and the people in it. This will help the students build expectations for listening.

2. Listening

Play the tape and have the students try the listening task. You may wish to stop the tape after each item, to check comprehension or to replay the segment.

3. Follow Up

Check the answers. Find out if the students misunderstood any parts of the tape or task and retry those sections.

Pair Practice

1. Preview of Language Key

The Language Key is highlighted to show to the students the kinds of expressions they will need to do this exercise with language accuracy. Model these expressions and explain any unknown vocabulary or grammar. The students should repeat each sentence.

2. Modeling

Students are to work with a partner. A students must look at the A page only; B students must look at the B page only. Each exercise involves a basic information gap: A and B must exchange information mutually in order for them to accomplish the goal of the task. Be sure that the students understand this procedure. Have two volunteers begin the exercise while the other students watch and listen. If necessary, have the whole class act as the A student for number 1 and you can take the role of the B student.

3. Free Practice
Allow ample time for all of the students to practice the activity and to complete the task. Give a time limit to make the outcome more important and to focus the students' attention on meaning.

4. Extra! Extra!
The Extra! Extra! activity at the bottom of the page is an open-ended speaking practice. You may have the students who finish early go directly to this exercise, or you may allot time for all students to try it.

5. Checking
Check that the students have completed the task. Ask questions and review the key grammar points. If time permits, try a Follow Up activity.

Social Talk

1. Listening
Have the students listen to the tape, or to the teacher, as they read the cartoon bubbles. You may wish to have the students repeat the lines. Point out to the students any features of the situations that are of interest. Elicit from the students any questions they might have.

2. Oral Practice
Have the students practice the situations in pairs. Each student should practice both parts of the conversations. After the students have practiced, some of the student pairs can present their conversations to the whole class.

Unit Notes

These Unit Notes provide suggestions for Warm Up and Follow Up activities to accompany each section of every unit.

INTRODUCTION UNIT (pages vi–viii)

This unit can be used in your first class meeting and periodically throughout the first few weeks of your course. The Introduction Unit consists of nine sets of items for the students to learn through listening and repetition.

1. Letters of the alphabet
Most of your students will know the English letters, but some may have problems with pronunciation. Special problems: G-J, B-V, D-T, G-Z, E-I, F, Q, W, Y.

Follow Up:
Write some place names on the board (*Tokyo, Seoul, Taipei, Los Angeles*). Ask the students to spell them aloud.

2. Numbers
Most of your students will know how to say the numbers in English, but many will have problems thinking of the numbers in English.

Follow Up:
Say some simple arithmetic problems to the class (*9 plus 7, 20 minus 8*). Ask them to say the answers.

3. Colors

Some students will have difficulty remembering some of the color words. Special problems: orange, blue, yellow, brown.

Follow Up:
Point to some items in the room. Ask: *What color is it?*

4. Time

Most students will have difficulty saying and understanding times in English. Special problems: noon–midnight, a.m.–p.m., when to say "o'clock."

Follow Up:
Use two pencils (or other long, thin objects). Hold up the two pencils to show different clock times (for example, both pencils pointing up is "12:00"). Make several different times. The students should say the times.

5. Days
Follow Up:
Hold up a large calendar for the current month. Point to a day. The students should say the day (Monday, Friday, etc.)

6. Months
Follow Up:
Ask several students: *When is your birthday?* or *When is (name of holiday)?*

7. Years
Follow Up:
Ask some questions: *When was (famous event)?* Then ask the students to try asking you some questions like this.

8. Dates
Follow Up:
At the start of every class day, ask one student to write the date on the board: Day, Month, Year.

9. Classroom expressions

It is important for you to use English as much as possible in the class. It is also important for the students to begin to use English for classroom directions and questions.

Follow Up:
Make a large poster with these expressions on it. Post it in the front of the class. Every time a student needs one of the expressions, point to the expression on the poster.

UNIT ONE (pages 1–8)

This lesson is about greetings and about describing people—their ages, nationalities, and relationships. Throughout the unit, try to keep your students focused on these basic ideas.

Visuals:
If possible, decorate the classroom with pictures or posters of 1. people greeting each other, 2. family trees and family photos, 3. world flags, 4. addressed envelopes from different countries.

Objectives:
• Present and practice basic greetings
• Present and practice basic descriptions of people
• Practice simple pair interactions

First Try (page 1)
Warm Up: Teacher and students
Take the first part in all of the dialogues, with the students, as a group, taking the second part. This will provide a clear example and will encourage all of the students to speak.

Follow Up: Good to see you!

Greet each student: *Hello, (name). Good to see you.* Shake hands with the students. Then ask all of the students to stand up and greet each other in English.

Word Bank (pages 2-3)

Warm Up: Pictures

Bring in magazine pictures of scenes from different parts of the world. Hold up one of the pictures. Ask the students: *Where is this picture from?* You may also try this with pictures of flags: *What country is this flag from?* Point out the difference between names of countries (e.g. *This flag is from Japan)* and nationalities (e.g. *It's the Japanese flag*).

Follow Up: Class Directory

To give further practice with writing addresses and phone numbers, pass a sheet around the class with these headings: *name, address, phone number.* Ask the students: *Please fill this out.* Then make copies of this "class directory" for each student in the class.

Easy Listening (page 4)

Warm Up: Left or right?

For each item (numbers 1–6) describe one of the two pictures (for example: *Number 1 It's a man*). The students should say *left* or *right* to show they can identify the correct picture.

Listening Dictation (page 5)

Follow Up: Compare

After listening, have two students write the sentences on the board. Ask the class to compare: are both correct? Encourage the students to find the errors without your help.

Listening Task (page 5)

Follow Up: Photos

Bring in photos or slides of your family or friends or former classmates. Show the pictures. Begin: *I'm going to show you some pictures of my (family).* Say one or two sentences about each person. For example: *This is Lisa. She's my sister. She's 21 years old. She lives in Florida.* Encourage the students to ask questions about each person.

Pair Practice (pages 6 and 8)

Warm Up: Countries

Bring in some magazine pictures of famous people from different countries. Hold up each picture. Ask questions about the pictures.

Follow Up: Introductions

Have several students introduce a classmate, based on the information they learned in the Extra! Extra! activity. You may write this frame on the board: This is _____. She's a _____ (job). She has _____ people in her family. Her favorite movie is _____. Her favorite food is _____.

Social Talk (page 7)

Warm Up:

Have the students look at the pictures. Point to each picture. Ask this question about each picture: *Where are they?*

Follow Up: In your language

Ask your students: *Do you know any similar expressions? Do you have expressions like this in your native language?* (For each situation) *What do you say in your native language?*

UNIT TWO (pages 9–16)

This lesson is about identifying items (*Whose is it? Where is it?*), quantities (*How many?*), and qualities *(Is it (old)?*). Throughout the unit, try to keep your students focused on how to describe items.

Visuals:

If possible, obtain some additional materials related to these themes. For example, you may ask your students to bring in one or two unusual things (such as momentos from trips) to place around the classroom. For each item, make a sign to describe it (for example: *This is Mari's. It comes from Thailand. It's green and gold. It's beautiful!*).

Objectives:
• Practice basic descriptions of things
• Practice asking questions about things
• Practice "goodbye" expressions

First Try (page 9)
Warm Up: Is this yours?
Walk around the classroom and pick up or point to items near the students. Ask questions to individual students: *Is this your...?* Encourage students to answer: *Yes, it is* or *No, it isn't.*

 Follow Up: Stand up
Ask several pairs of students to act out their original dialogues. Ask them to stand and to use actual props.

Word Bank (pages 10–11)
Warm Up: What's this in English?
Find out how many words the students already know. Point to different items in the classroom and ask: *What is this?* (or *Do you know what this is in English?*).

Follow Up: Rooms
To give more practice with the vocabulary, bring in some pictures of different rooms. Hold up a picture. Ask the students to describe: *What's in this room?*

Easy Listening (page 12)
Warm Up: True or false?
 Use two books, two pencils, and two notebooks. Put different combinations of these items on your desk (for example, one book, two pencils, one notebook). Make some statements (for example: *There is one book, one pencil, and two notebooks on my desk.*). Students should say *true* or *false*.

Listening Dictation (page 13)
Warm Up: Point
Say the words and phrases in the box in a random order. Ask the students to point to the word or expression you say.

Listening Task (page 13)
Follow Up: Covered objects
To provide extra practice, try a game of "covered objects." Bring several pictures (cut out from magazines, for example). These may be pictures of people, places, animals, or any common objects. Cover the pictures with the paper. Slowly, pull up the sheet of paper. Who can guess what it is the soonest?

Pair Practice (pages 14 and 16)
Follow Up: In this picture
Do the activity in the Extra! Extra! section with the whole class. Bring in a large picture. Hold it up for one minute. Then place it face down on the table. Students should say one sentence: *There is... in the picture* or *There are ... in the picture*. Write down the sentences on the board. See how many sentences the class can make.

Social Talk (page 15)
Warm Up: Where are they?
Have the students look at the pictures. Ask some questions about the pictures: *Where are they (in picture 1)? Who are they (in picture 3, 4)? Are these people friends (husband and wife, co-workers, classmates)?*

UNIT THREE (pages 17–24)

This lesson continues with describing things and expressing possession (*I have... He has... They have...*).

Visuals:

If possible, have your students make some simple posters related to the theme of possessions. For example, you may ask students to create a small collage of three or four interesting (not expensive) items they own. The posters can be labeled with the name of the student, for example: *Kay has...* These small posters can be posted around the room.

Objectives:
• Practice basic descriptions of things
• Draw attention to singular–plural differences
• Practice functions of offering and accepting offers

First Try (page 17)
Warm Up: It's nice!

Walk around the classroom and pick up or point to items near the students. Ask questions: *Is this your...?* or *Are these your...?* Encourage students to answer: *Yes, it is* or *Yes, they are.* Make a comment about each item or set of items, such as *It's (nice)*.

Word Bank (pages 18–19)
Warm Up: What's this?

Find out how many words the students already know. Point to different items in the classroom, including students' clothing items, and ask: *What is this?* (or *Do you know how to say this in English?*).

Follow Up: Which picture?

For extra practice, bring in several large pictures of individuals from magazines, tape them to the board, and number the pictures. Ask the students simple questions to elicit understanding of the vocabulary. For example: *Which one has a red shirt? Which one does not have a watch?* Students can show understanding by saying the correct number of the picture.

Easy Listening (page 20)
Warm Up: True or false?

Make several "true or false" statements about students in the class (*Mariko has a green sweater. Sunny has two black shoes.*). The students should say *true* or *false*.

Listening Dictation (page 20)
Follow Up: Pair dictation

Create a "pair dictation" practice by writing 6 similar items. (1. *Are these your suitcases?* 2. *Yes, they are.* 3. *Is her sweater new?* 4. *No, it isn't. It's old.* 5. *Is their house large?* 6. *Yes, it is. And it's expensive.*) In each pair, one student receives 1, 3, and 5 on a card. The other student receives 2, 4, and 6 on a card. They should read the sentences to each other. The partner writes the sentences.

Listening Task (page 21)
Follow Up: Dialogue

Use the tape to create a practice dialogue. Write this dialogue on the board.

Look, there's (Amy).
(Amy)? Where?
(She's) wearing (a red sweater).
Oh, yes I see (her).

Have the students practice in pairs for the people in the picture: Anne, Brenda, Carol, David, Edward, Frank.

Pair Practice (pages 22 and 24)
Warm Up: Similar pictures

Draw two similar pictures of a room on the board, using a room with simple items in it (cups, glasses, tables, chairs, windows, doors). Make four or five small differences between the pictures. Ask the students: *What's different?* Write a list of the items that are different.

Follow Up: In this picture

Do the activity in the Extra! Extra! section with the whole class. Use a different photograph (or painting) that is large enough for everyone to see. While the class is looking at the picture, you can say some sentences about the picture (for example: *There are two people in the picture*). Then when you cover up (or take down) the picture, ask about these items (for example: *How many people are in the picture?*).

Social Talk (page 23)

Warm Up: Where are they?

Have the students look at the pictures. Ask some questions about the pictures: *Who are they? Where are they?* You may need to introduce new vocabulary items: guest, customer, waiter.

Follow Up: Presentations

Allow several pairs to present their conversations to the class. Encourage them to take their time— to speak slowly and clearly, with the proper emphasis.

UNIT FOUR: CHALLENGE UNIT (pages 25–28)

This is an expansion unit. There are reviews of short conversations and the grammar of questions and answers. There is also a vocabulary game and an interaction activity.

Objectives:
• Review basic greetings and goodbyes
• Review and expand the question forms used in Units 1–3
• Practice group interactions and communication games

Conversation Review (15 minutes)

The purpose of this exercise is to review the Social Talk sections from Units 1–3. Have the students work in pairs. Each pair should make several short conversations using each table (Tables 1–3). Allow about 2–3 minutes for the students to practice each table.

Check this exercise by calling on several pairs of students to model dialogues for each table.

Follow Up: Response Game

Write each expression in the right column of the tables on an index card. Place the cards in the center of a table or post them on the board. Call out one of the expressions in the left column of the tables in the book. The first student to pick up (or touch) an appropriate answer card, and then say the response, gets a point.

Question and Answer Review (30 minutes)

This exercise may be done individually, in pairs, or as a whole class. It is best to do this as a guessing game, rather than a direct matching activity. Have the students read one item in the Answers column first. Then they are to think of a question for this answer. After they think of a possible question, they should try to find that question, or a similar one, in the Questions column.

Correct this exercise by having the students write both the questions and the answers on the blackboard.

Follow Up: Short Answers

Continue this activity orally. Give a short answer (for example: *No, I don't*). The students are to ask a question that will give that answer (for example: *Do you smoke? Do you live in New York?*).

Grammar Watch (10 minutes)

This exercise can be done individually. The students should check the correct sentence. Then they should identify the error and circle it.

Follow Up: Errors Game

Identify the grammar items in this quiz that your students have most trouble with. For each item, make two similar index cards, one with an error (for example: *This is Mary book./This is Mary's book.*). Post the cards side-by-side on the board. Have the students come to the board and remove the "error card."

Vocabulary Expansion (20 minutes)

This game can be played in pairs. Sometimes, more than one answer is possible. Students should attempt to explain the pattern—why they chose their answer.

 Follow Up: Patterns Game

Ask the students to work in pairs. Each pair should make five more items for this "patterns game." They can look at the Word Bank pages to find vocabulary items. Have each pair read one or more of their items aloud to the class. Who can guess the missing items?

Interaction Game—Favorites (30 minutes)

Explain the meaning of "favorite" (= likes most). Ask the students to read all of the questions aloud and to ask you the meaning of any items they do not know (e.g, *dessert, song, artist, program*).

Have the students work in pairs or groups of three. You can use dice or a pointer to determine the number of squares each player should move or flip a coin as suggested in the instructions. When a player moves to a square, he or she must ask the question to a partner. The partner answers and writes his or her initials on that square.

Set a time limit (suggested time limit: 15 minutes). At the end of this time, if no one has reached the goal, the player who answered the most *different* questions is the winner.

Follow Up: Favorites

Ask several students in the class one or more of the "favorites" questions. If they are able, ask your students to expand their answers with *because* (for example: *I like football because it's an active sport.*).

UNIT FIVE (pages 29–36)

This lesson is about people—what they do, where they live and work. Throughout the unit, help the students talk about and ask about people.

Visuals:

If possible, bring in pictures of famous people. Under each person's picture, write these questions with blank lines: *What's his (her) name? How old is he (she)? Where does he (she) live? What does he (she) do?* During the lesson, you can refer to these pictures to practice the language points.

Objectives:
• Practice asking questions about people
• Practice saying simple sentences about people
• Learn introductions

First Try (page 29)
Warm Up: Role cards
Make some simple, large "role cards" with a name (example: *Lena Smith*), and a residence (example: *San Francisco*). Give these cards to your students. Ask one of the students to stand up and show their role card. Students should ask: *What's your name?* and *Where do you live?* The student with the role card should answer. After several students have done this, point to the students with role cards and ask the class: *Who's that? Does she live in San Francisco?*

Word Bank (pages 30–31)
Warm Up: Work scenes
If possible, bring in pictures of work scenes and different jobs. Ask the students: *Where is this?* Point to a person in the picture and ask: *What does she (or he) do?* Write any new words on the blackboard.

Easy Listening (page 32)
Follow Up: Complete it
Say the first part of each pair of sentences (from the tape). Have the students say the second sentence. (For example, the teacher says: *She teaches at Central High School.* Students say: *She's a teacher.*)

Listening Dictation (page 32)
Warm Up: Left or right?
Write these sets of words in two columns on the board: *Does he / Does she; Where does he / Where does she; Is she / Is he; What do / What does; Do they live / Where do they live; Are you / Are they*. Say one member of each pair. The students should call out *left* (column) or *right* (column) to identify which one they heard you say.

Listening Task (page 33)
Follow Up: Famous people
To provide extra listening practice about occupations, bring in photos of some well-known people. Hold up each picture and ask questions such as: *What's her name? Where does she live? (Do you know where she lives?) What does she do?*

Pair Practice (pages 34 and 36)
Warm Up: What do they do?
Put a picture of a famous person on the board (with tape or magnets). Below the picture, write: *WORK (What does she do?):* _____ and *RESIDENCE (Where does she live?):* _____. Gesture for the students to ask you the questions. Give answers. Write the answers on the board. Tell the students that the Pair Practice for today is like this.

Social Talk (page 35)
Warm Up: What's happening?
Have the students look at the pictures. Ask some questions about the pictures: *What is happening?* (Someone is introducing a friend.) Encourage the students to answer in English.

Follow Up: Introductions
Have the students stand up and practice introducing other students. The minimum number for each group should be three (as in the model dialogues), but if there are four or more, the person introducing the new person should name all the people in the group (*Mary, I'd like you to meet Jesse, Sue, and Tim*).

UNIT SIX (pages 37–44)

This lesson is about schedules and daily activities (*When do you get up? How is your new job?*). Throughout the unit, try to keep your students thinking about how to talk about their schedules and daily routines.

Visuals:
If possible, bring to class some additional materials related to these themes. You might ask each student individually to bring in a magazine picture for each of the actions in the Word Bank section: get up, eat breakfast, go to work, etc. Post these around the room.

Objectives:
• Practice talking about schedules
• Learn to use time and frequency expressions
• Practice asking for and giving assistance

First Try (page 37)
Warm Up: Questions
Have the students look at the pictures (1-4). Ask some questions to emphasize the term *a new (job, car, class, bicycle)*, such as, (for number 1) *He has a new job. What is it?* (He's a police officer.) (For number 2) *What are they talking about?* (Her new class.) (Number 3) *What does he have?* (A new car.) (Number 4) *What does he have?* (A new bicycle.)

Word Bank (pages 38–39)
Follow Up: How many?
Ask the class to continue Exercise number 3 by suggesting new verb phrases to use (for example: *take the train to class, come to class late*). Take a survey of the whole class, for example: *Do you eat dinner with your family? How many always eat dinner with your family? How many usually...?* etc. Write the numbers on the board.

Easy Listening (page 40)
Warm Up: Repeat

Say the verb expressions for each picture. Have the students repeat the expressions. This will help them anticipate what is on the tape.

Listening Dictation (page 40)
Follow Up: Blank Dictation

Ask the students to write on a separate paper. Try a "blank dictation." Use the same (or similar) sentences to those in the dictation. The students are to write the "blank" words you say. For example, if you say: *Andy blank up at 7 o'clock*, the students should write "gets." If you say: *Andy blank up blank 7 o'clock*, they should write "gets, at."

Listening Task (page 41)
Follow Up: Daily Activities

Write several verbs on the board for the students' daily activities: *get up, eat breakfast*, and so on. Give the students time to write a short paragraph about their daily schedule. Collect the paragraphs and read some aloud to the class, using third person. (*Sam gets up at 6:30. He eats breakfast at 7:00. He usually has...*) Read the paragraphs with correct grammar if the students have made errors.

Pair Practice (pages 42 and 44)
Warm Up: Vocabulary Preview

Write the two names (Tim Rourke and Marla Mitchell) on the board. Under each name, write the activities (make breakfast, have a meeting, etc.) in random order. Make sure that your students understand the meaning of these terms.

Follow Up: Everyone does...

For the Extra! Extra! activity, ask the students to find three activities that "match" for them and their partner. Then ask each pair to say one activity. (For example: *We both watch the TV news every day*.) Can you find one activity, as a class, that everyone does every day?

Social Talk (page 43)
Follow Up: What do you say?

Ask the students: *Do you have expressions like these* (e.g. "Excuse me", "I'm sorry", "Oh, really?") *in your native language? Do you use them in the same way? If not, what do you say in your native language?*

UNIT SEVEN (pages 45–52)

This lesson is about locations and descriptions of people and things. As you go through this unit, try to keep your students' attention on accuracy of descriptions.

Visuals:

If possible, post a large chart which shows objects in different positions (on top of, in front of, etc.). See the Word Bank page for a list of location expressions. You may also find (or make) and post a large aerial map of a section of your city for practice with locations.

Objectives:
• Learn the basic expressions for locations
• Practice describing locations
• Practice function of asking for favors

First Try (page 45)
Warm Up: Where is...?

Write the expressions for locations on the board: *in front of, next to, between, behind.* Draw arrows to show the meaning. Ask about where some students are: *Where's (Keiko)?* Elicit from students, while pointing to the board, *She's in front of _____. She's behind _____.* and so on.

Word Bank (pages 46–47)
Warm Up: Locations

Ask several questions about the location of objects in your room. You can ask two types of questions: 1. *Where's the (pencil sharpener)?* or 2. *What is on the right side of (my desk)?*

Follow Up: What is...?
Write these adjectives on the board: *expensive, cheap, beautiful, large, small*. Ask, *What (in this room) is expensive?* How many things can the students say?

Easy Listening (page 48)
Warm Up: Picture Description
Write: *There is... There are...* and *in front of, under, on, next to, between* on the board. Ask the students to say some sentences about the picture using these expressions.

Listening Dictation (page 48)
Warm Up: Guessing
Ask the students to read the sentences with the blanks. Can they guess the missing words?

Listening Task (page 49)

Warm Up: Follow along
To prepare your students for this long listening extract, describe the picture as your students follow along but don't use the names. For example: *There's a man standing next to the table. Do you see that man? And there's a woman in front of the picture. Can you see her?* and so on.

Follow Up: Picture description
Write these words on the board: *standing, next to, in front of, sitting, couch, man, woman, another*. Ask one of the students to describe the picture orally. (For example: *Andy is standing next to the table...*)

Pair Practice (pages 50 and 52)
Warm Up: Activities
If possible, bring in a picture with a lot of characters and a lot of activity. (The *Where's Waldo?* series of books are very useful for this.) Display the picture (perhaps on an OHP) and ask some questions such as: *Is there a man with a cane in this picture?* Wait for the students to identify the person. After you have done this for several items, write these sentence frames on the board: *Is there a .... in the picture? Are there two ....(s) in your picture?* This will help prepare the students for the pair activity.

Follow Up: Changes
Do the Extra! Extra! activity with the whole class. Arrange several items on your desk. Then have the students look away while you change some of the positions of the items. To get the items "correct", the students must make a complete grammatical sentence. (For example: *Now the book is on the right side of the desk.*)

Social Talk (page 51)
Warm Up: Questions
Have the students look at the pictures as you ask some questions. Number 1: *Where are they?* Number 2: *Why does she need help?* Number 3: *What's the problem?* Number 4: *What does she have?*

Follow Up: In your language
Ask the students: *Do you have expressions like these (Can you do me a favor?) in your native language? How do you say this in your native language?*

UNIT EIGHT: CHALLENGE UNIT (pages 53–56)

This is an expansion unit. There are two grammar review activities and four language games.

Objectives:
• Review grammar patterns from the previous units
• Review and expand vocabulary from the previous units
• Practice group interactions and communication games

Question and Answer Review (30 minutes)
This exercise may be done individually, in pairs, or as a whole class. Correct this exercise by having the students write both the questions and the answers on the blackboard.

Follow Up: Short answers
Continue this activity orally. Give a short answer (for example: *Every day.*). The students are to ask a question that will give that answer (for example: *How often do you speak English?*).

Grammar Watch (10 minutes)

This exercise can be done individually The students should check the correct sentence. Then they should identify the error and circle it.

Follow Up: Errors game

Identify the grammar items in this quiz that your students have most trouble with. For each item, make two similar index cards, one with an error (for example: *They live London/ They live in London.*). Post the cards side-by-side on the board. Have the students come to the board and remove the "error card." Make this into a game by having teams: the first team to remove the error card gets a point.

Vocabulary Game—Word Images (30 minutes)

This game can be played with teams of up to ten people. If the game moves too slowly, give a time limit for drawing (suggested: 30 seconds). To make the game more challenging, the team members should not look at their books to see the possible words. You may also give a "guess limit" (suggested: maximum of five guesses). If a team cannot guess the word within the time limit, the other team can have one guess. If they guess correctly, they receive the points. Play the game until every student has a chance to draw on the board.

Follow Up: Word cards

Make cards with these words and other words that the students have been adding to their New Words lists.

Language Game—Guess what? (15 minutes)

Warm Up: Demonstration

Demonstrate this activity by saying: *I'm thinking of something in this room. It's brown and it's big and it's next to the door.* (Your desk.) Try other, more difficult examples (such as, a drawer in your desk, someone's necktie, a note card on someone's desk, a pin on someone's shirt).

After all of the students understand the directions, have them form groups of four. The purpose of the game is to keep the others guessing. To keep score, each guess counts as one point for the "thinker." The person with the highest total wins.

Follow Up: Vocabulary review

On the board, list all of the new vocabulary items that were used during the game.

Language Game—Maps (20 minutes)

This activity can be done in groups of four, or in pairs, if that is more convenient.

Warm Up: Demonstration

Demonstrate this game by saying: *Look at your map. Is there a (bank) near here?* After the students say: *Yes,* ask: *Where is it?* The students should say: *It's on First Street.* Try one or two more examples until you are sure everyone understands. Then ask them to practice in groups of four.

Interaction Game—Personal Information (30–40 minutes)

Warm Up: Personal questions

With books closed, ask the students: *What are some personal questions?* To get the students started, you might write one or two (such as: *Where do you live? What's your phone number?*). Try to get as many questions as possible. Write them on the board.

To make the game more challenging, you may add some rules: 1. Players should answer with complete sentences to receive a point. 2. Players should write their initials on a square when they answer correctly. 3. You cannot stop on a square with initials on it.

UNIT NINE (pages 57–64)

This lesson practices the present progressive verb form. Throughout the unit, focus the students' attention on verbs and correct use of verb forms.

Visuals:

If possible, obtain some additional pictures which will illustrate verbs. For example, you may ask your students to bring in one or two magazine or newspaper pictures, each of which shows an action clearly. Post these pictures, with a large label showing the verb.

Objectives:
• Practice use of present progressive forms
• Increase active use of vocabulary to talk about actions
• Learn language for requests

First Try (page 57)
Warm Up: New vocabulary
Use pictures (cut out of magazines) which show people doing different actions. Hold up each picture and ask: *Where is she (he)? What is she (he) doing?* Write down new vocabulary items on the board. Encourage the students to focus on the -ing endings.

Word Bank (pages 58–59)
Warm Up: What are they doing?
Find out how many words the students already know. Point to different actions in the picture and ask: *What's he (she) doing?* Remind the students to use the -ing endings as they answer.

Easy Listening (page 60)
Warm Up: Picture preview

Have the students look at the pictures on the right. Point to a picture and ask: *What is she (or he) doing?* After the students answer orally (for example: *He's eating a sandwich*), write the answer on the board.

Listening Dictation (page 60)
Follow Up: Dialogue strips
Prepare the two conversations (beginning *Is Mr. Rainer in his office?* and *Is Lara in the kitchen?*) on strips of paper. Jumble the ten strips of paper and place them on a table. Ask the students to sort out the two conversations and to put the lines in order. Then have them check their answers by looking in the book.

Listening Task (page 61)
Warm Up: Picture questions
To prepare your students for this long listening extract, describe the picture and ask questions about it. (Don't use the names of the people.) For example: *Look at this building. How many floors are there?* (Six) *Look at the top floor, the fifth floor. There's a man. He's sitting. Is he busy?* (No.)

Pair Practice (pages 62 and 64)
Warm Up: Silhouettes
Cut out some pictures from magazines—pictures of people doing different actions. Make dark photocopies so that only an outline "silhouette" remains. Hold up each silhouette. Can your students guess the action? Encourage the students to answer with -ing forms (*They're singing*). Explain that the pair practice for today is similar to this guessing game.

Follow Up: I'm thinking of someone
Do the activity in the Extra! Extra! section with the whole class. You may begin: *I'm thinking of someone in this class.* Gesture for the students to ask you questions. Remind the students to use only Yes/No questions. The student who guesses the person then continues.

Social Talk (page 63)
Warm Up: Requests
Give some simple requests to individual students: *Can you open the door? Can you hand me that book? Can you put this tape into the tape player?* Vary the forms somewhat: *Would you mind...? Could you...? Please... Will you...?* After giving several examples, write some of the "request forms" on the board.

UNIT TEN (pages 65–72)

This lesson introduces language for shopping, particularly for food items. During the lesson, focus on accurately describing quantities.

Visuals:
If possible, bring in advertisements from supermarkets, which often show the "counters" (package, box, etc.) and generally show the price. Look at the items on the Word Bank pages for ideas. You may also want to bring in large, full color pictures of different food items.

Objectives:
• Practice functional language used for shopping
• Learn the basics of count and non-count nouns
• Learn new vocabulary related to food

First Try (page 65)
Warm Up: Food items
Hold up pictures of food items (or, if possible, actual food items): a few apples (or other "countable" fruits), a bag of rice, a milk carton. Write this question frame on the board: *Do we need any* _____? Hold up the food items and have the students ask this question for each item. Point out that non-countable items (such as rice, bread, milk) do not take an -s ending.

Word Bank (pages 66–67)
Follow Up: Typical day
Ask the students to write on the board all of the food items they eat (or drink) in a typical day or week. Then ask them: *(About) How much* _____ *do you eat in one day (or one week)?* Write down the "counters" they need to give their answers. (For example: *one cup of coffee, two bowls of rice, one-half carton of milk.*)

Easy Listening (page 68)
Warm Up: Store map
Have the students look at the map of the store. Point out and model the pronunciation of the following: Aisle (or Lane)1A, Aisle 2B, the front of the store, the back of the store. Also model the pronunciation of the food items: *fish, ice cream*, and so on.

Listening Dictation (page 68)
Warm Up: Guessing
Ask the students to look at the sentences before listening to the tape. Can they guess the words in the blanks?

Listening Task (page 69)
Warm Up: Count or non-count?
Before playing the tape, ask the students which items on the list are "count" and which "non-count" items. For the non-count items (milk, rice, bread), ask what "counters" might be used.

Pair Practice (pages 70 and 72)
Warm Up: How many?
Demonstrate the basic arithmetic needed to do this exercise: Say: *I need 12 oranges, but I only have 3 oranges. How many should I buy?* (9) *That's right. 12 minus 3 is 9. I should buy 9 oranges.*

Follow Up: Something unusual
Continue the Extra! Extra! activity by asking your students: *What is something unusual (or strange) that you bought last week?* Ask several students.

Social Talk (page 71)
Warm Up: Which one?
Have the students look at the pictures. Ask some questions about the pictures: *Where are they? Who (which one) is the clerk (waiter)? Which one is the customer?*

UNIT ELEVEN (pages 73–80)

This lesson focuses on the past tense. Throughout the unit, help the students focus on past tense forms in both statements and questions.

Visuals:
Bring in pictures of people doing identifiable actions: buying something, eating something, having a

meeting, driving, watching TV. Below each picture, attach a large sign showing a past time: last night, yesterday, last week, one hour ago, on March 1st, 1993. Post these around the room as reminders of past tense expressions.

Objectives:
• Practice use of past tense in questions and statements
• Learn common irregular past tense forms of verbs
• Practice responding to news items

First Try (page 73)
Warm Up: Past forms
Have the students look at the "thought bubbles" in each illustration. Ask: *What are they talking about?* (the hospital, home, Washington, a shopping mall). Then ask: *Where was she (he) yesterday?* Focus on the past form: *She was (at the hospital).* On the board, write two columns: *Present, Past.* In the Present column, write "is"; in the Past column, write "was." You can then use these columns as you go through the model dialogues.

Word Bank (pages 74–75)
Follow Up: Did you...?
To practice the past tense, ask several students some Yes/No questions, such as: *Did you walk to school today?* Have them answer with complete sentences (*Yes, I walked to school today* or *No, I didn't walk to school today.*).

Easy Listening (page 76)
Warm Up: Describing
Ask the students to look at the pictures. Can they describe the action in each picture in the past tense? (She played tennis, She visited an art museum, and so on.)

Listening Dictation (page 76)
Follow Up: Blank dictation
Ask the students to write on a separate paper. Try a "blank dictation" which focuses on verb tenses. Use the same or similar sentences to those in the dictation. The students are to write the "blank" words you say. For example, if you say: *I blank to the beach yesterday*, the students would write "went." If you say: *I blank to the beach every Sunday*, the students should write "go."

Listening Task (page 77)
Follow Up: True or false?
After correcting the task, make some "true or false" sentences. (For example: *Roger played golf on Friday.*) The students should answer "true" or "false." If the answer is "false," they should try to make a true sentence (for example: *He played golf on Monday.*).

Pair Practice (pages 78 and 80)
Follow Up: Last week
Try the Extra! Extra! activity with the whole class. Can you find something that everyone (or nearly everyone) did last week?

Social Talk (page 79)
Warm Up: Personal News
Ask several students individually about some "personal news." For example: *How is your new job going? How are your other classes? How are things at home?* After each student has answered, give a comment, such as: *Oh, I'm glad to hear that.* or *Oh, I'm sorry to hear that.* Then explain that the Social Talk in this unit is about this kind of "personal news."

Follow Up: Guess what?
Elicit from the students some actual "personal news" that any of them would like to share with the class. Then make some conversations based on this news: *Guess what? (Name) got a new job! Oh, that's great (interesting, too bad, a surprise)!*

UNIT TWELVE: CHALLENGE UNIT (pages 81–84)

This is an expansion unit. There are reviews of the grammar of questions and answers, two language games, and a Social Talk review activity.

Objectives:
- Review the functional language from the Social Talk sections in the book
- Review of key vocabulary items from the book
- Practice group interactions

Question and Answer Review (30 minutes)
This exercise may be done individually, in pairs, or as a whole class. Correct this exercise by having the students write both the questions and the answers on the blackboard.

Follow Up: Matches
Write each expression in both the right and left columns of the tables on index cards. Place the cards in the center of a desk or post them on the board. Have the students find matches for questions and answers. This can be played as game by forming teams to compete for the most pairs.

Grammar Watch (10 minutes)
This exercise can be done individually. The students should check the correct sentence. Then they should identify the error and circle it.

Follow Up: Errors game
Identify the grammar items in this quiz that your students have trouble with. For each item, make two similar index cards, one with an error (for example: *Yesterday I buy some fish. / Yesterday I bought some fish.*). Post the cards side-by-side on the board. Have the students come to the board and remove the "error card." Make this into a game by having teams: the first team to remove the error card gets a point.

Vocabulary Game—Containers (20 minutes)
This activity can be done with individuals or in teams. You can make this activity into a game by setting a time limit (suggested: five minutes). You may also add more items to increase the challenge. See how many students have classified all items correctly in this allotted time. Write out the correct answers on the board when everyone has finished.

Warm Up: What's in it?
Ask the students to close their books. Write the container words on the board: jar, can, box, carton, bottle, bag. Ask the students how many food items they know for each container. You may wish to have the students work with a partner for several minutes to generate their lists. Write the foods under each container name.

Vocabulary Game—What's the word?
Warm Up: Demonstration
Demonstrate the game by acting out one or two of the verbs for the whole class. Who can guess the action?

Follow Up: Definitions
Prepare short definitions for each word. Have the students close their books. Say your short definitions of the words. For example: *You are her brother. She is your* _____. Can the students guess the words?

Interaction Game—Responses (20–30 minutes)
Demonstrate the game before class with several students. Those students can then be "group leaders" to teach the game to the rest of the class.

You can make the game more interesting by having dice to determine how many squares to move. You can increase the challenge of the game by adding this rule: You cannot give a response that another player has already given.

Follow Up: What did you say?
Ask several students to give their own responses to some of the statements in the board game. See how many variations were said by the students in the class.

Acknowledgements

I would like to thank the many individuals who assisted me in the course of developing of *Real Time English* and *Prime Time English*:

Damien Tunnacliffe for his initial vision and direction
Tim Hunt for his encouragement during the planning stages
Gill Negus for her direction in the production stages
Helena Gomm for her steady attention and enduring vigor throughout the project
Eden Temko for her clarity and amiable humor during the final stages of editing
The Design Department, especially Nicola Witt and Helen Locker (Design Locker), and Neil Adams (D.P. Press) for their creativity and aplomb in designing the books
The Art Editors, Hilary Fletcher, Marilyn Rawlings and Veena Holkar, and the Production Controller, Donna Wright
David Briscoe and the A-V department for their resourcefulness in producing the tapes
The staff of the American English department at Longman Group UK, particularly Louise Elkins, and to the other publishers and editors, especially Nicola Gooch, who helped give life to the books.

Shinsuke Suzuki of Longman Japan, for his valued personal and professional guidance
The staff of Longman Japan, particularly Hiromi Tsuchiya, Steve Martin, Steve Galloway, Hideki Komiyama, and Takashi Hata for their congenial support
Kevin Bergman for his wise counsel on the project from start to finish.

Dugie Cameron of Longman Asia Pacific for his insistence on inclusiveness and high standards of development
Joanne Dresner and Debbie Sistino of Longman Publishing Group in the USA for their valuable input on many aspects of the project
Many others within the Longman Group worldwide, particularly Jill Wang and Jung Ja Lee, for their openness and generosity in offering suggestions.

Valerie Randall for her wit and sharp conceptual ability in developing the dialogues

The teachers who reviewed or piloted earlier versions of the books in their classes, for furnishing clear feedback and suggestions on ways to improve them:

Harumi Adachi
Rudi Besikof
Carmen L. Casagnanos
DeWitt Conklin
Teresa Cox
Tomoko Fujita
Nobuko Hara
Ken Hartmann
Marc Helgesen
Junko Kurata
Ken Kitazawa
Chris Lynch
Hiromi Matsumoto
Mariko Miura
Sian Munekini
Mie Okada
Jeremy Palmer
J. Saul Ray
Leslie A. Rice
Cheryl Richmond
Hung-En Seng
Izumi Seo
David Shaw
Eric Strickland
Hisae Suzuki
Miho Takagi
Yoichi Takagi
Junko Tanikawa
Keiko Thompson
Tom Werner

My family, Keiko, Ammon and Leon Rost, for helping me with numerous bits of language research, and for providing the humor, warmth, and sustenance needed during this marathon.

M.R.

We would like to thank the following for their permission to reproduce copyright material and photographs:

Ace Photo Agency for pages 62 (above right) and 64 (above right); Allsport UK Limited for page 34 (above left); Art Directors Photo Library for pages 31 (below), 78 (below) and 80 (below); J Allan Cash Photo Library for page 75 (left); Colorific/Michael Grecco for page 3 (below right), /Terence Spencer for page 3 (below left), 33 (above right) and Dough Menvez Picture Group 34 (centre left); Greg Evans Photo Library for pages 6 (above left), 8 (above left), 78 (above) and 80 (above); Harper Collins for page 33 (below left); The Image Bank/Kevin Forest for pages 6 (above right) and 8 (above right); Japanese Embassy for page 3 (above right); Network/ M.B.Camp/MATRIX for pages 6 (centre left) and 8 (centre left); PhotoEdit for pages 6 (centre right) and 8 (centre right); Redferns/Mick Hutson for pages 62 (lower centre left) and 64 (lower centre left); Rex Features for pages 3 (above left, above centre, below centre), 33 (above left), 33 (below right), 34 (above centre, above right, centre centre, centre right, below left, below centre left, below centre right), 36 (above centre, above right, centre centre, centre right, below left, below centre left, below centre right), 62 (upper centre right, below right), 64 (upper centre right, below right) and 94; Tony Stone Worldwide for pages 6 (below left, below right), 8 (below left, below right), 62 (above left, upper centre left, lower centre right, below left), 64 (above left, upper centre left, lower centre right, below left), 75 (right), 78 (centre) and 80 (centre); Telegraph Colour Library for page 31 (above).

The photographs on pages vii, 19 (bicycles and sweaters) and 39 (2.30pm clock) were taken by John Birdsall; pages 7, 15, 23, 35, 43, 51 above left, above right, below right, 63, 71, 79 above left, above right and below right by Gareth Boden; page 31 centre by Geoff Howard; page 59 by Peter Lake; page 39 by Longman Photographic Unit (6pm clock); pages 19 (except bicycles and sweaters), 22, 24, 39 (four clocks), 51 below left, and 79 below right by Neil Phillips of Pinsharp.

Illustrated by Richard Adams, Noel Ford, Neil Gower, Bill Gregory, Pauline Hazelwood, Tim Kahane, Maggie Ling, Frances Lloyd, Colin Mier, Sharon Scotland and Bob Warburton.

Cover illustration by Rosemary Wood

Addison Wesley Longman Limited
Edinburgh Gate, Harlow, Essex CM20 2JE, England
and Associated Companies throughout the world.

First published 1994
Fifth impression 1996

Set in 12/13.5pt Monotype Amasis by DP Press Limited, St Julians, Sevenoaks, Kent TN14 0RX

Produced by Longman Singapore (Pte) Ltd
Printed in Singapore

ISBN 0 582 09221 3